INTERNATIONAL EXPRESS

PRE-INTERMEDIATE
Teacher's Resource Book

Liz Taylor

with contributions to the Resource file by Imogen Arnold,
Gillian Carless, Jane McKinlay, Jacqui Robinson

OXFORD UNIVERSITY PRESS

Course overview

Introduction

Learner needs

International Express Pre-Intermediate is a course for adult professional learners. These learners

- need English as a language of international communication in both professional and social contexts
- need to review and build on the grammar they have already covered
- need to develop fluency and accuracy
- need to extend and develop their active and passive vocabulary
- have limited time available for study
- can develop strategies to enable them to take control of their own learning.

Course aims

International Express provides

- clear learning aims, targeted to learners' needs
- the grammar, vocabulary, and functions necessary for learners to become operational in a range of professional and social situations
- a new approach to grammar which guides learners to work out rules of meaning and usage, supported by clear, easily accessible grammar summaries and reference material
- strategies for effective vocabulary learning
- materials adapted from authentic sources, to reflect learners' needs and expectations.

Rationale

Syllabus and approach

The grammatical, lexical, and functional content of the course is targeted specifically to meet those needs which adult professional learners have in common. The choice of items, and the order in which they are introduced, is determined by frequency, and usefulness to the learners' operational needs.

Grammar items are presented in realistic contexts, chosen to reflect both meaning and use. Learners analyse data and examples from listening or reading texts, and are then guided to work out rules. The accompanying Pocket Book is used in class, to verify conclusions, and is also a reference source.

Vocabulary development

Vocabulary development is especially important for learners at this level. Each unit has a topic which provides a natural context for the grammar, vocabulary, and functions introduced. Topics are chosen for their interest and usefulness, and develop the learner's range of key vocabulary. In addition, the Wordpower section of each unit presents effective strategies for organizing and learning vocabulary.

Social English

Key functional exponents, selected for their high frequency and usefulness for common professional and social situations, are presented, to enable learners to increase their confidence in dealing with those situations. The focus is on interaction, on both initiation and response.

The exponents present a separate situational syllabus, linked by theme and topic to other sections of the unit.

Teacher's Resource Book

The Teacher's Resource Book has two main sections:
- Unit overviews and teaching notes
- Resource file

Unit overviews and teaching notes

The overviews provide a quick reference to the topics, stages, and activities of each of the four main sections of a unit – Language focus, Wordpower, Skills focus, and Social English. They give a brief description of each stage, and show where taped material and the Pocket Book are needed. They also show the first point where Resource file material can be used.

The teaching notes have been written with both the experienced and the less experienced teacher in mind. The detailed, step-by-step guide to teaching each unit is designed for the less experienced teacher in particular. The experienced teacher also may find the other material in the teaching notes useful.

The notes include some background information about topics; key vocabulary needed for each activity; warnings about possible areas of difficulty, indicated by the symbol ⚠ ; suggestions and ideas for extra practice and follow-up activities. Answers to the exercises in the Student's Book, and a full tapescript, are incorporated.

Resource file

The Resource file is a source of photocopiable material which can be used either as extension or consolidation material, or for revision. Both the unit overview and the detailed teaching notes indicate the first point at which a piece of material can be used.

Materials in the Resource file are organized into files: Grammar, with additional practice activities, and grammar games with cards which aim to develop students' understanding and use of tenses; Vocabulary, with material for regular and systematic reviews of the key vocabulary in each unit; Skills, with texts adapted from authentic sources to provide additional vocabulary and skills work, and a variety of role-play, discussion, and speaking activities; and Social, with activities to review the functional language from the Social English sections.

There are two additional files which are not directly linked to the Student's Book and which can be used as appropriate. These are the Situations file, which has practice for situational areas not covered in the Student's Book – at the doctor's, at the bank, etc.; and the Writing file, which gives models and task practice for basic letter-writing – asking for information, booking, etc.

There are also three tests, which can be used after Units 4, 8, and 12.

The Resource file has brief instructions for activities where these are necessary, and a photocopiable answer key. The index to the Resource file gives the reference number for each activity, the language point focus, title, and the first place in the Student's Book where it can be used.

Teacher's Resource Book: contents

Student's Book: Unit structure

Each unit has four sections. The sections are linked by topic, and are designed to follow on from one another. Wordpower and Social English have their own developmental syllabus, to enable them to be followed as a separate strand, if necessary.

Language focus presents and practises the target grammar in a context related to the general topic of the unit. It has four stages.
1 An introductory activity which sets the scene for the presentation topic. This activity aims to stimulate interest, to find out what learners already know about the topic, and to introduce and check vocabulary. It is either a brief discussion stimulus – questions, photos, or a cartoon – or extracts which give vocabulary and background information to the topic. It is designed as a whole class activity.
2 Presentation of the target grammar in a realistic context, a listening or reading text related to the topic of the unit. Comprehension is checked by questions or a transfer task.
3 Grammar analysis, which focuses on examples of the target grammar from the presentation text, and guides learners towards formulating rules. Learners are then referred to the grammar summaries and reference material in the Pocket Book.
4 Practice. This provides a series of activities, moving from controlled to freer practice, designed to enable learners to gain fluency and confidence in using the target grammar. There is a variety of individual, pairwork, and group work activities, which maximize opportunity for intensive practice. This stage ends with a group activity which provides an opportunity for freer communicative practice, followed by a feedback activity such as a mini-presentation.

Pronunciation is included in each unit. This section has either discrete item pronunciation practice, or work on stress, rhythm, and intonation. Learners are asked to identify and discriminate, then practise particular points linked to the focus of the unit. It aims to raise awareness.

Wordpower presents and activates a lexical set or semantic field related to the topic of the unit. At the same time it introduces a variety of strategies for organizing and learning vocabulary effectively, which learners can use independently. It has two stages.
1 Introduction of topic-related vocabulary, demonstrating a particular vocabulary learning strategy.
2 A follow-up practice activity, to activate the vocabulary introduced.

Skills focus has longer listening and reading texts, adapted from authentic sources, which provide further exposure to the target grammar of the unit and develop listening, speaking, reading, and writing skills. It has four stages.
1 A preview to introduce and stimulate interest in the topic, through a quiz, discussion, short text or questionnaire.
2 A task or tasks to complete while reading or listening. This might involve finding the answers to the preview quiz, completing a chart, or preparing questions for other students.
3 Follow-up. These are pairwork and group work communicative activities such as discussions, writing tasks or presentations, designed to activate new vocabulary and to build confidence.
4 A project, which suggests ideas for further work relating to the topic of the listening or reading text, and which can be prepared in or outside class.

Social English presents and practises basic key phrases which adult professionals need for socializing and telephoning. To provide continuity, and a clear context, the Social English dialogues develop a scenario involving a number of characters. There are two main stages.
1 A range of possible exponents is presented. Students then identify the exponents being used in a recorded dialogue.
2 Controlled, then freer role-play. This provides the opportunity to build fluency and confidence.

Student's Book contents

Approaches: working with *International Express*

The adult learner

Adult learners have experience, knowledge, skills, and abilities which can be put to good use in the language learning situation. The tasks and activities in *International Express* require learners to take responsibility, to initiate, to make decisions. Handing over responsibility, whether for working out a rule, for deciding on effective learning strategies, or for running a group activity, can have a very positive effect on learners' confidence, and is an essential part of enabling learners to become operational. Effective learning is guided by the teacher, but the learner is encouraged at all times to be independent.

Grammar

The approach taken in *International Express* encourages learners to think about meaning, analyse examples, and complete rules in order to discover the concepts and use of different grammar structures. Learners are guided to use language as data from which they can work out rules and concepts for themselves.

Your students may be unfamiliar with this approach to grammar, so at the beginning of the course, work with them as they complete the rules in the grammar section, questioning and prompting them so they understand how they can use data to work out rules of meaning and usage. The teaching notes give suggestions for using examples of the target structure in the Language focus listening and reading texts to guide students, and of the questions you might ask in the early stages.

At the end of each grammar section, use the grammar summaries and tables in the Pocket Book to check and confirm with your students the hypotheses they made. Encourage them to use the Pocket Book regularly, to review and to find information they need.

Group activities

The group work tasks in *International Express* are designed to be done as 'students in charge' activities. As a general rule, put students in charge of group activities as often as possible, so they get used to leading this part of the lesson. Make sure they understand their role and responsibilities first, then hand control over to them. In group discussions, for example, appoint a student as chairperson in charge of the discussion, instead of leading the discussion yourself.

All learners need to understand very clearly what they have to do in group activities. Explain the task clearly and set a time limit where appropriate. During the preparation stage, walk round and check progress, helping where necessary, but let the students take control of the activity whenever possible. This can be very motivating as it increases involvement in learning and enables the learners to make use of their own skills and experience.

There are many opportunities in *International Express* for students to make presentations, present results, or give feedback at the end of a group task. If an overhead projector is available, give students transparencies so they can prepare a presentation.

When the students are in control, take a back seat so students no longer focus on you as the person in charge. Monitor students' use of language and do remedial work on mistakes later. Remember also to give positive feedback. Praise students for what they did well, both in terms of their use of language and the way in which they carried out the task.

Feedback and correction

Students need feedback on the language they produce, but the amount of correction, and the techniques used, depend on the stage of the lesson and the learners' needs. It is important that your students know when you will correct them, and you may want to spend time at the beginning of the course agreeing with them when and how they can expect correction and feedback. Always give the student who made a mistake the opportunity to self-correct, then invite correction from other students. If no one can correct the mistake, give the correction, check students understand it and get them to repeat the correct version.

In whole class activities in the Language focus and Practice stages of the lesson where you are working on the target structure in a controlled exercise, correct on the spot. In group work and freer practice activities, on the spot correction may interfere. Intervene in such activities only when help is needed or when communication breaks down. Use the Monitor sheet in the Teacher's Book Resource file to make a note of the most important mistakes, and do remedial work on the mistakes later. Write the mistakes on the whiteboard, or give students photocopies of the Monitor sheet. Students then work in pairs or groups and try to correct the mistakes. You may also like to give each student a blank Monitor sheet where they can note down corrections.

Vocabulary

Wordpower presents and practises a variety of strategies for organizing and remembering vocabulary. Encourage your students to experiment with different strategies, and allocate time in class to discuss how effective they find them. Encourage learners to decide what is the most efficient strategy for them. They are provided with a range of strategies and techniques to choose from.

The teaching notes for each lesson suggest the vocabulary which needs to be checked at a particular point. Depending on your students' needs, decide whether you want to teach the vocabulary for active use, or for passive understanding. For active use, elicit or explain the meaning, and ask check questions to make sure students have understood. Then provide practice contexts in which students can use the new vocabulary and practise the pronunciation. Encourage your students always to record active vocabulary. Some vocabulary needs only to be checked in order that it does not interfere with understanding.

Review vocabulary regularly. There are vocabulary sections in both the Review Units and the Tests, and regular vocabulary reviews in the Teacher's Resource file.

Organizing group work and pairwork

There is a variety of individual, pairwork, and group work activities in *International Express*. In very small classes you may prefer to do some of these activities as whole class activities, rather than divide students into pairs or groups. It is important for the stages of a lesson to have a variety of both activity and interaction patterns, however, and putting students into pairs or groups gives them more opportunity to speak. It also encourages students to work with each other and creates a classroom atmosphere in which learners expect to learn from each other as well as from the teacher.

Some pairwork activities are in two stages, to maximize the communicative value of the task, and to give students the opportunity to work with a number of people. Students first work together as AA, BB pairs, for example, to prepare questions for a survey. They then change partners and form AB pairs for the second stage of the activity, in this case to carry out the survey.

Role-play activities, whether done in pairs or in groups, can often benefit from being done in three stages. In the first stage, the students prepare what they are going to say, and practise while the teacher monitors. There is then a feedback stage, where students discuss any problems and the teacher gives advice and suggests alternatives. In the final stage, the students carry out the role-play.

Pronunciation

The approach to pronunciation is designed to raise awareness of particular elements, and to encourage learners to identify patterns and work out rules for themselves.

One-to-one courses

International Express can be used for one-to-one courses with very little adaptation. All the pairwork activities can be done if the teacher takes the role of the other person in the pair. Many of the group activities which come at the end of Practice and Skills focus, for example, discussions, presentations, interviews, and Projects, are appropriate in one-to-one teaching situations. ■

UNIT 1

Language focus   p. 2

Present Simple, Frequency adverbs

1   Discussion: international fairs.
2   Deducing information from business cards.
3,4 Listening: introductions at a conference.   1.1, 1.2 ⬤⬤
     Grammar analysis 1: Present Simple.   p. 2 📙

Practice   p. 3

1   Sentence completion.
2   Question words.
3   Write questions for answers.
     Pronunciation: intonation of closed and   1.3 ⬤⬤   p. 10 📘
     Wh- questions.
4   Pairwork: question and answer.   1.1,1.2 📕
5,6 Group work: read information and prepare
     questions for another group. Answer questions.   p. 6 📘
7   Pairwork: question practice.
     Grammar analysis 2: Frequency adverbs.
8   Rewrite sentences.
9   Pairwork survey: leisure.
10   Writing: personal profile.   p. 9 📘

Wordpower   p. 6

Personal information, leisure pursuits

1-3 Organizing vocabulary: topic groups, word
     groups, word maps.
4   Recording meaning: alternative methods.   1.3 📕
     Asking for help with vocabulary.   p. 10 📘

Skills focus   p. 8

Reading. English as an international language

1   Languages quiz.
     Magazine article about English: check quiz answers.
2   Pairwork: prepare and write a memo to recommend
     a language programme.
3   Project: International English words.   1.4 📕

Social English   p. 9

Introductions, greetings, and goodbyes

1   Warmer: discussion.
2-4 Introductions   1.4 ⬤⬤
5   Saying goodbye.   1.5 ⬤⬤   1.5 📕
6   Role-play: introductions and saying goodbye. p. 17 📙   1.6 📕
                                                              p. 11 📘

     📙   Pocket Book

     📘   Workbook

     📕   Resource file

<table>
<tr><td>

Needs analysis

</td><td>

</td></tr>
</table>

Language focus

Vinexpo, the International wine and spirits exhibition, is one of the most important international exhibitions and meeting places for people in the wine and spirits business. It takes place in Bordeaux, France, every two years.

1 Look at the pictures. Encourage students to speculate about what is happening. Prompt with questions: *Do you attend trade fairs? Which ones? Are they important for your business?*

2 Look at example. Elicit two more sentences from cards: *works in..., is a...,* etc. In pairs, students make two sentences from each business card.

⚷ (Possible answers) Roberto is a wine consultant. He works in Florence.
His telephone number is 055 53 75 866.
Bresson Translation Services has offices in London, Paris, and Rome.
James is a wine journalist.
He works in London.
His office is in Honeywell Street.

1.1 ▣ **3** Students read through questions for Dialogue 1.
- Play Dialogue 1.
- Students check answers in pairs. Play tape again if necessary.
- Follow the same procedure with Dialogues 2 and 3.
- Check answers, whole class.

⚷ 1 No, he doesn't.
2 How do you do. How do you do.
3 She is with the Vinexpo translation service, to translate for a group of Italian wine producers.
4 What do you do?
5 Because he has a job for her.
6 At 7 o'clock that evening.

Note: introductions and greetings are dealt with in the Social English section of this unit, p. 9.

1.2 ▣ **4** Focus question: *Why does James need a translation agency?*
- Play tape through once. Check answer to focus question.
- Check vocabulary: *sales conferences, interviews, presentations*
- Look at example question and answer.
- Check students understand *underline,* and understand the task.
- Give students time to read through questions, and answer if they can.
- Play tape again if necessary.
- Students check answers in pairs.
- Check answers, whole class.

⚷ 1 interviews people   2 two or three times a year   3 London

Present Simple
As students may be unfamiliar with this approach to grammar, explain that in this section of each unit they will work with data from the listening or reading texts in Language focus. This will enable them to work out and clarify grammar rules for themselves.
- Read through examples, whole class.
- Elicit completion of first rule. Check understanding by asking students to find an example of a long-term situation (*She lives in London/She has a translation business*) and a routine activity (*They visit Vinexpo/He often travels to France*).

⚷ Use the Present Simple to talk about long-term situations and routine activities.
- Encourage students to look for differences in form, with prompt questions if necessary: *What happens to the verb after 'he'? In the negative, what word follows 'I'? What word follows James?* etc.
- Students complete rules in pairs.

• **Check answers, whole class.**

To make the question, use *do + I/you/we/they +* infinitive.
The positive form always ends in *-s.*
To make the negative, use *does + not +* infinitive.
To make the question, use *does + he/she/it +* infinitive.

Refer students to Pocket Book p. 2. Explain how students can use this as reference material throughout the course, in and out of class.

Practice ❶ **Students complete sentences individually. Check answers and pronunciation, whole class.**

1 writes	3 meet	5 don't speak
2 doesn't import	4 doesn't live	6 travels

❷ **Look at pictures. Elicit question words.**
• **Practise questions.**

1 Who?	3 What?	5 Which?
2 When?	4 Where?	

❸ **Students write questions in pairs.**
Position of *for* in example, and *about* in 6.
• **Check answers, whole class.**

1 Where do they live?	4 When does she visit them?
2 How often does he go there?	5 Who do they meet at Vinexpo?
3 Where do they meet?	6 What does he write about?

Pronunciation **Read example questions aloud. Draw attention to arrow indicating intonation patterns of a. (rising at the end) and b. (falling at the end).**

1.3 ① **Play the tape. Students write a. or b.**
• **Play tape again. Pause after each question and check answers.**

1 a.   2 b.   3 a.   4 b.   5 a.   6 b.   7 b.   8 a.   9 b.   10 b.

1.3 ② **Play tape again, pausing after each question for students to repeat.**

③ **Students complete pronunciation rule in pairs. Check answer, whole class.**
In questions that begin with question words, the voice goes down at the end.

---

❹ **Look at example, whole class.**
• **Students change roles after five questions.**
• **Ask follow-up questions:** *What does James write about? Which magazine does James write for?*

1 Does Monique speak Italian? Yes, she does.
2 Where does she work? In London, Paris, and Rome.
3 Do James and Roberto write about wine? Yes, they do.
4 Does James work for *Wine and Dine*? Yes, he does.
5 Does Roberto know Monique? Yes, he does.
6 Does James live in Italy? No, he doesn't.
7 Does he love his work? Yes, he does.
8 Does James go to France and Italy? Yes. Two or three times a year.
9 Where do Monique's parents live? Near Dijon.
10 Does she travel to Paris? Yes, she does.

Resource file 1.1, 1.2

❺ **Check vocabulary: (Editor's letter)** *spirits, key people, to rate wines* **(Visitor profile)** *to commute, a vineyard*
• **Divide students into groups to read texts and prepare questions. Make sure they know they have to exchange questions, so should write them on pieces of paper and legibly!**

@ **Group A** (Possible questions)
Which magazine is the letter from?
What does James do?
Does he often travel in Europe?
Who does he interview?
What are his hobbies/interests?
Which sports does he play?
Does he enjoy English cooking?

Group B (Possible questions)
Why is Monique at Vinexpo?
Which stand is she on?
Does she live in Paris?
Does she know a lot about the
  wine business? Why?
Where do her parents live?
Where is her father from?
What are her hobbies/interests?

6 Students exchange questions, and refer to text for answers.
Follow-up activity Ask students to make true/false statements about James Turner and Monique Bresson. Elicit correction of false statements.

7 Allow time for students to think of questions (but not to write) before they begin pairwork.

Frequency adverbs
- Use diagram to check meaning of frequency adverbs.
- Encourage 'active' reading of examples. Prompt with questions if necessary: *Where's the verb? What's the main verb?* etc.
- Explain that *sometimes* can go at the beginning or end of a sentence for more emphasis.
- Students complete rule. Check answer, whole class.

@ We write words like *always/usually/never* after the verb *to be* but before other verbs.

8 Students rewrite sentences individually.
- Check answers, whole class.
Follow-up activity Students write three more sentences, some true, some false. They read out sentences and others guess if true or false.

9 Give students time to think of the two extra questions before they begin the interview.

10 Before students begin their profiles, elicit and write a model on the board, drawing attention to the use of *and* and *but*. *Marco often plays tennis at weekends, but he rarely goes to the theatre. He sometimes eats at a restaurant and he often travels by plane...*
- Collect the Visitor profiles students have written about their partners. Read some to whole class. Ask class to guess which student the profile describes.
Follow-up activity Play Twenty Questions. Tell students you are thinking of a famous person. They can ask you 20 questions to find out who the person is, but you can only answer *yes* or *no* to their questions.

Wordpower

The Wordpower section for this unit introduces a range of possible ways of organizing and recording vocabulary and is designed to raise awareness of the variety of possible methods.

Organizing vocabulary
Discuss how students already organize and learn vocabulary, and list on board. Explain that the Wordpower sections of this book will give them practice in a range of strategies. Prompt with questions: *Do you write down vocabulary? When? How? In a notebook?* etc.

1 Students complete the topic groups in pairs.
- Check answers, whole class.
@ (Possible answers) Family: daughter, aunt, married.   Flat/House: lounge, bedroom, garage, kitchen.   Jobs: dentist, firefighter, actor, farmer, secretary, artist.
- Students ask and answer questions in pairs to practise vocabulary. *Do you have any children? Do you live in a flat?* etc.

2 Complete the word groups, whole class.
- Students ask and answer questions in pairs to practise vocabulary. *How do you travel to work?* etc.

to live in a house/a village/ a town
to work part-time
to go to work by car/by train/by underground
Students match words in pairs.
- **Check answers, whole class. Elicit other nouns which go with the verbs.**

 go to the cinema   read newspapers and magazines
listen to music   watch TV
play tennis

3 **Students complete the word map in pairs.**
- **Draw the word map on the board. Check answers.**

Interests: cinema, photography, reading, music.
Sports: swimming, walking, tennis.

Word maps are a useful way to organize vocabulary. They will be used again in Wordpower in later units.

Recording meaning
- **Give students time to read suggested methods. Check which ones they already use. Ask which they would like to try.**

4 **Students work in pairs to discuss ways to record the meaning of the words in the list.**
- **Compare suggestions, whole class.**
- **If you feel students need further practice, use words from first page of Wordpower section and discuss what information they could record.**
- **Stress the importance of reviewing vocabulary regularly in a systematic way.**

Ask for help
Ask questions to practise. Use unfamiliar words and speak quickly so students have to use phrases to ask for repetition and explanation. *Do you know any wine merchants? Does Monique work freelance? Is James Turner a member of a union?* etc.

RF Resource file 1.3

Skills focus **1** Before Languages quiz, write the title *English: the language of millions* on the board.
- **Elicit ideas of what the text is about. If time, write up ideas on the board to check after reading.**
- **Give time limit for students to do quiz. Explain that the answers to questions 2 and 3 are in the text.**
- **Check vocabulary:** *job advertisement, subsidiary, employee, border*
- **Students read text.**
- **Check answers, whole class.**

 1 (Possible answers) Australia, Canada, New Zealand, South Africa, UK, USA
2 a. about 350 million
3 umbrella   Italian   quartz   German
marmalade   Portuguese   cargo   Spanish
élite   French

2 Give pairs time to brainstorm ideas.
- **Before they begin to write, check memo format and write outline on board.**
- **Discuss organization of memo: they should outline the situation, present possibilities and reasons, and make suggestions.**

If students are unfamilar with the use of memos, explain that they are a very straightforward means of communication. They should be written in a clear and simple style, and do not need any special language formulae.

3 **Check vocabulary. Point out that international words are often false friends.**
Parking in English is the activity, not the place, which is *car park* in the UK and *parking lot* in the USA. *Un smoking* is *a dinner jacket* in the UK and *a tuxedo* in the USA.
- **Brief follow-up discussion on the use of international words in students' languages.** *Do they use many? Are they useful?*

 Resource file 1.4

Social English ❶ Discuss each question, whole class.

    1 With monolingual groups, find out what students know about hand-shaking customs in other countries, so they can compare them with customs in their own country.

⊙⟶ Usually, people in Britain only shake hands when they meet for the first time, or when they meet again after a long time.

    2 Practise useful phrases: *Could you repeat your name, please?* and *Sorry, I didn't catch your name.*

⊙⟶ I'm sorry, I didn't hear your name.
Could you repeat that/say that again, please?

    3 Ask students to imagine they are giving this information to a foreign visitor. Compare with own language if appropriate.

    ● Practise with prompts: *What do you say when you meet someone in the morning? When you leave someone in the evening?*

⊙⟶ *Good morning/Good afternoon/Good evening* are greetings. We say
Goodnight to say goodbye/end a conversation at night.

❷ Students read through list and underline expressions individually.
    ● Check answers, whole class. Draw attention to the use of *How do you do* for introductions only, and *How are you?* for greeting someone we know.

⊙⟶ 1 Excuse me, are you...?   2 How do you do.   3 Let me introduce you to...
    May I introduce myself, I'm...   I'd like to introduce you to...
                                                                    Pleased to meet you.

1.4 📼 ❸ Play tape once. Students tick the phrases they hear.
    ● Check answers, whole class. Practise pronunciation.

⊙⟶ 1 Excuse me, are you...?   2 Nice to see you   3 I'd like to introduce you to...
    May I introduce myself? I'm...   again.   Pleased to meet you.
                                              How's the family?

❹ Students work in pairs to match phrases.
    ● Check answers, whole class. Practise pronunciation.
    ● Practise in pairs with right column covered until students are confident of responses.

⊙⟶ How are you?   Very well, thank you. And you?
How are you?

Pleased to meet you.   Pleased to meet you, too.
How do you do.   How do you do.
Please call me James.   Then you must call me Luigi.
How's life?   Not too bad, but very busy.
Hello, are you Roberto?   Yes, that's right.

1.5 📼 ❺ Play tape once.
    ● Students check answers in pairs.

⊙⟶ I must go now.   I really enjoyed meeting you, too.
It was very nice meeting you.   Have a good trip back.
I look forward to seeing you.   Thank you, and the same to you.

    ● Play all four dialogues again. Pause tape after each sentence. Individual students repeat. Drill pronunciation of individual words and sentence intonation.

⚠ *I look forward to see**ing** you,* not *to see you. I enjoyed meet**ing** you.*

 Resource file 1.5

❻ Allow time for students to think of reasons for attending the conference. If necessary, model by taking one role yourself.
    ● Make sure students move around and practise introducing themselves and other people, greeting people, and saying goodbye, with as many people as possible. Walk round monitoring and helping.

📖 Refer students to Pocket Book p. 17. Explain that each Social English section has a summary in the Pocket Book.

 Resource file 1.6

Tapescript Unit 1

1.1
R=Roberto, J=James, M=Monique

Dialogue 1

J Roberto! Good to see you again. How are things?

R Oh, hello, James. Fine, thanks – very busy – lots of work, lots of travelling as always. Can I introduce a good friend of mine, Monique Bresson? Monique, this is James Turner.

M How do you do.

J How do you do.

Dialogue 2

J Are you an importer?

M No. A translator. I'm here with the Vinexpo translation service. I'm with a group of Italian wine producers who don't speak French.

R Monique is a genius, James. She speaks five languages fluently.

J Really? Which ones?

M Spanish, Italian, and Hungarian, and of course French and English. What do you do?

J I'm a wine consultant, like Roberto. We both write about wine; I'm a journalist with *Wine and Dine* magazine.

Dialogue 3

J Actually, I have a job for someone who speaks English and Italian. Are you free later to discuss it?

M I'm not sure at the moment. I'm afraid I already have several appointments today. Perhaps this evening. How about seven o'clock in the main bar?

J Fine.

1.2
M=Monique, J=James

J Ah, Monique.

M Sorry I'm late.

J That's OK. A glass of champagne?

M Thank you. So, what does a wine journalist do?

J Well, I go to the wine regions and I interview people in the business to get information for my articles. I travel to Italy two or three times a year.

M Do you enjoy your job?

J Yes, I really love my work, especially the travelling. I meet so many interesting people.

M I enjoy travelling, too…

J Yes, I see from your business card that your translation agency has offices in Paris, London, and Rome. Where do you live?

M In London. But I often travel in Europe and I come to Paris regularly, usually for work. Sometimes I come to visit my parents. They live near Dijon. So, why do you need a translation agency?

J Well, to help with interviews for my book about Italian wines.

M Oh, really? How interesting. We have a lot to discuss!

J Yes, we do. Do you have time for dinner? The lobster really is excellent.

M Thank you very much.

1.3

1 Do you travel a lot?

2 How often do you come here?

3 Do you speak French?

4 How often do you go to Italy?

5 Do you work here every year?

6 Who do you meet here?

7 Where does he live?

8 Does James speak Italian?

9 What does Roberto do?

10 Which languages does Monique speak?

1.4

Dialogue 1

T=Tony, M=Monique

T Excuse me, are you Ms Bresson?

M Yes, that's right.

T May I introduce myself? I'm Tony White. How do you do.

M How do you do, Mr White.

Dialogue 2

J=Jeanne, R=Roberto

J Roberto! Nice to see you again. How are you?

R Hello, Jeanne. Fine, thanks. How are you? How's the family?

J Oh, very well, thank you, Roberto.

Dialogue 3

R=Roberto, L=Luigi, J=James

R James, I'd like to introduce you to Luigi Bastini. He represents some growers in the Chianti area of Italy here at Vinexpo. Luigi, this is a journalist friend of mine, James Turner.

L Pleased to meet you, Mr Turner.

J How do you do. Please call me James.

L Then you must call me Luigi.

1.5

M=Monique, J=James

J Monique, I must go now. It was very nice meeting you, and I look forward to seeing you in London next month.

M I really enjoyed meeting you, too, James. Have a good trip back.

J Thank you, and the same to you. Bye.

M Bye. See you soon.

UNIT 2

Language focus   p. 10

Present Simple and Present Continuous

1   Discussion: department stores.
2   Reading: a Harrods Director describes
     his work.
3   Write questions about the text.   p. 12 WB
     (Present Simple review.)
4   Identify verb forms in text.

     Grammar analysis: Present Simple and
     Present Continuous.   p. 2,3 PB

Practice   p. 11

1   Identify use of tenses.
2   Gap-fill: description of someone's work. 2.1, 2.2 RF
3   Role-play: explanations on the phone.
     Pronunciation: /s/, /z/, or /ɪz/ endings
     in Present Simple.   2.1 ▭ p. 15 WB
4   Pairwork: question and answer about
     previous texts.
5   Pairwork survey: job descriptions.   p. 13 WB

Wordpower   p. 13

Collocates of work and job

1   Using information from a dictionary.
2   Complete collocations.   p. 16 WB

Skills focus   p. 14

Listening. Numbers, shopping

1   Reading numbers aloud: review.
2   Interview about Harrods: complete
     information sheet.   2.2 ▭
3   Company information: prepare and
     give presentation.   2.3 RF
4   Project: prepare an article or information
     sheet about an organization.   2.4 RF

Social English   p. 16

Telephoning: making contact and leaving messages

1, 2 Telephoning: leaving a message.   2.3 ▭
3   Guided role-play: leaving a message.
4   Complete conversation.   2.4 ▭ p. 18 PB
5   Discrimination exercise.   2.5 ▭
6   The alphabet: pronunciation and spelling.
7–10 Practice: numbers and the alphabet.   2.5, 2.6 RF
                                                p. 17 WB

1 Look at pictures. Ask students to talk about any of the stores, or one they know. Prompt with questions: *Do you shop in department stores? Which one? Why? What do you like about it? What don't you like about it?*

Bloomingdale's, in New York, is one of the oldest and most famous department stores in the USA. El Corte Inglés has 3 stores in Madrid, and other stores throughout Spain, with around 56,000 employees.

2 Check vocabulary with questions: *In which department do you buy men's clothes? Children's clothes? Things for children to play with?*
- Explain that answers to questions 1 and 2 can be worked out from the text.
- Students read text.
- Check answers, whole class.

1 A *customer* is a person who buys goods or services, usually from a shop or company.
A *buyer* is a person whose job is to choose and buy the goods which large shops sell to their customers.
A *supplier* supplies the goods which shops sell to their customers.
2 A *collection* is a group of new products, usually of fashion clothes, e.g. *summer fashion collection*.
3 He sees his secretary, the buyers, and the sales staff.
4 Yes, he is.

3 Students work in pairs to write questions.
Position of *to* in 5.
- Check questions, whole class.

1 What does she give him?
2 Who does he meet?
3 Who do they visit?/What do they attend?
4 How often does he walk round his departments?
5 Who does he talk to?

4 Students work in pairs to find sentences in text.
- Write headings on board: *A typical day, This month*. Write students' suggested sentences under headings and elicit answer.

(Possible answer) I have a lot of meetings./I'm having a lot of meetings.
The sentence about Manfred's typical day is in the Present Simple tense. The sentence about Manfred's work this month is in the Present Continuous tense.

Present Simple and Present Continuous
- Give students time to read through examples.
- Draw attention to time expressions: *this month, at the moment, at present, currently*, in the examples of the Present Continuous.
- Students complete grammar rules in pairs.
- Check answers, whole class.

Use the Present Simple to talk about regular activities, and the Present Continuous to talk about current activities.
To make the Present Continuous, use *am/is/are* + *-ing* form of the verb.
- Check form of the Present Continuous in negative, question, and contractions.

 Refer students to Pocket Book p. 3.

Practice **1** Point out importance of time expressions in deciding regular (R) or current (C) activities.
- Students mark sentences individually, then check in pairs.
- Check answers, whole class.

1 R   2 R   3 C   4 R   5 C   6 R   7 C   8 C

2 Students complete description individually.
- Check answers, whole class.

1 works   3 phone   5 is speaking   7 enjoys   9 is organizing   11 are filming
2 spends   4 ask   6 is giving   8 meets   10 are making   12 want
- Ask follow-up questions for further practice: *Where does Peter work? Who does he spend a lot of time with? What is he doing today?*

 Resource file 2.1, 2.2

③ Check vocabulary in box.
- Model example with two students.
- Students can sit back-to-back for telephone conversation.

🔑 Miss Adams   She's giving a presentation to the sales staff.
Mr Smith   He's visiting our London office.
Mr Kurtz   He's making a phone call to Paris.
Mrs Li   She's attending a conference.
Ms Engel   She's seeing a customer.
Dr Brown   He's/She's having lunch with a supplier.

Pronunciation   **①**   Write phonetic symbols /s/, /z/, /ɪz/ on board. Read the three example sentences aloud.
- Students identify the three sounds they hear.

🔑 /paːks/   /draɪvz/   /fɪnɪʃɪz/

2.1 📼 **②**   Play tape once. Students tick sounds.
- Play tape again. Pause after each verb and check answers.

🔑 1 drives /z/   3 discusses /ɪz/   5 spends /z/
2 visits /s/   4 speaks /s/   6 finishes /ɪz/

2.1 📼 **③**   Choral and individual repetition.

---

④ Refer back to texts. One student asks about Manfred, the other student asks about Peter. Give them time to prepare four or five questions.
- Students ask and answer questions in pairs.

⑤ Read through examples. If necessary, elicit questions for topics 5 and 6 on form, focusing attention again on use of Present Simple for regular activities, Present Continuous for current activities.
- Students prepare questions in pairs (AA, BB), then change partners for the interview (AB, AB).

If there are students in the class who do not have a job, they should be the interviewer, not the interviewee for this pairwork. Alternatively, students not in work answer as Monique Bresson, James Turner, Peter Willasey, etc., and use their imagination!

🔑 (Possible questions)
1 When do you start/finish work?
2 What time/Where do you usually have lunch?
3 Do you sometimes have a lot of meetings?
4 How often do you make phone calls in English?
5 Do you generally make a lot of business trips?
   Are you making any business trips this month?
6 Do you generally meet many visitors?
   Are you meeting any visitors this month?
7 How many days' holiday do you have each year?
   Where do you go for your holidays?
8 Do you do many training courses?
   Are you doing any courses at the moment?
9 What projects are you working on currently?
10 Do you enjoy your job? Why/Why not?
11 How often do you use a computer?
12 How important is English in your work?

Wordpower   The dictionary extracts in this section are from the *Oxford Dictionary of Business English* and the *Oxford Wordpower Dictionary*.

❶ Match the first sentence with whole class, as example.
- Students match other sentences individually, then check answers in pairs.

🔑 1 2   2 1b.   3 1a.   4 1b.   5 1a.   6 3
- Write *work* on board. Ask students to look at blue box and find words we often use with *work*. Explain that we call words we often use together *collocates*.

- Explain synonyms = *words which mean the same*. Ask students to find examples of synonyms in blue box.

❷ Students use second dictionary extract to complete tables in pairs.

⊙⟿ to apply for a job
to find a job
He's got a part-time/permanent/temporary/well-paid job.

- Explain that dictionaries help with additional information about meaning and use of words.

Follow-up practice Whole class. Students ask each other questions to practise the different meanings of *work*. Elicit questions: *How do you travel to work? What work do you do?* etc.

Skills focus **❶** Draw attention to the use of *and* after *hundred*: *a hundred and fifty*; and no '*s*' after *two hundred*, *three thousand*, *four million*, etc. Point out the use of a comma, not a full stop, for 1,000, 3,000,000, etc. in the UK and the US.

⊙⟿ a. a/one hundred
b. a/one hundred and fifty
c. a/one thousand
d. three thousand five hundred
e. twenty thousand
f. thirty thousand five hundred
g. a/one million
h. ten million

- Write more numbers on board to give more practice.

2.2 **❷** Check vocabulary in press information sheet.

- Play the interview once.
- In pairs, students discuss and note the information they remember.
- Play tape again. Students complete information sheet.
- Students check answers in pairs.
- If necessary, play tape again. Pause tape and check answers.

⊙⟿ 1 250 kinds of cheese   180 sorts of bread and patisserie   100 tons of chocolate
2 4,000 years ago
3 70% of its own electricity   11,500 light bulbs   30,000 customers
   300,000 customers
4 £1.5 million on an average day
5 £9 million for the first day

Follow-up activity Discuss with students the information about Harrods and what they think about it. Does it surprise them?

❸ Students work in groups to prepare a short talk. Suggest they either divide their talk into sections and each present one section, or appoint a spokesperson to give whole talk.

RF Resource file 2.3

❹ Students could present their press information sheet/article on an OHP transparency, or on the board.

RF Resource file 2.4

Social English **❶** Find out if students use English on the phone.

- Elicit phrases they know for making contact, leaving a message, etc. Prompt with questions: *You're phoning someone. The receptionist answers. What do you say? What do you say if the person isn't there?* etc.

2.3 - Play tape. Students complete message pad.
- Check answers.

🔑 Message for   Monique Bresson
    Caller's name   James Turner
    Company   *Wine and Dine* magazine
    Number   0171 331 8579
    Please call.

2.3 🔲 **❷** **Students read through phrases. Elicit who uses each phrase, caller or person receiving call.**
- **Play tape again. Students tick phrases they hear.**
- **Students check answers in pairs.**

🔑 Could I speak to Monique Bresson, please?
Who's calling, please?
Hold the line, please.
I'm sorry. She's in a meeting.
Can I take a message?
Could you ask her to call me?
- **Practise pronunciation. Remind students of intonation in *Wh-* and closed questions.**

❸ **Elicit possible phrases, whole class, if necessary.**
- **Students practise in pairs, back-to-back. Change roles.**
Follow-up activity In pairs, students role-play calling and leaving messages for other members of the group.

2.4 🔲 **❹** **Before listening, students complete as much of conversation as they can.**
- **Play tape to check answers.**

🔑 1 speak   2 calling, please   3 It's   4 the line

2.5 🔲 **❺** **Play tape once.**
- **Students check answers in pairs.**

🔑 1 b.   2 b.   3 a.   4 b.
- **Play tape again, if necessary.**

❻ **Write the letters (*a, e, f, i, o, r, u*) on board, and practise pronunciation of the key words (*say* to *who*) and letters.**
- **Students work in pairs to complete chart.**
- **Check answers, whole class.**

🔑							
/eɪ/ (as in **say**)	a	h	j	k			
/iː/ (as in **she**)	e	b	c	d	g	p	t	v
/e/ (as in **ten**)	f	l	m	n	s	x	z
/aɪ/ (as in **fly**)	i	y					
/əʊ/ (as in **go**)	o						
/aː/ (as in **bar**)	r						
/uː/ (as in **who**)	u	q	w				

❼ ❽ ❾ **Students practise in pairs.**

❿ **Students cover up information while they ask questions.**
- **Students can also exchange their own or their company addresses, telephone and fax numbers, if they like.**
Follow-up activity Dictate phone numbers, spellings, etc. whole class.

RF   Resource file 2.5, 2.6

Tapescript Unit 2

2.1

1 drives
2 visits
3 discusses
4 speaks
5 spends
6 finishes

2.2

P=Peter, I=Interviewer

I Tell me, Peter, what makes Harrods so famous?
P Well, it's the biggest department store in the UK – and its Food Hall and Egyptian Hall are very famous. People come to Harrods just to see them.
I What is special about the Food Hall?
P It sells many different kinds of food. For example, it has 250 kinds of cheese from all over the world, and more than 180 kinds of bread and patisserie, which 36 pastry chefs prepare every day. Customers also love all the different kinds of chocolate. They buy 100 tons every year.
I That's amazing! And why is the Egyptian Hall so famous?
P Well, when people see it they feel they're in another world. It looks like an Egyptian building from 4,000 years ago and it sells beautiful objects. They're not 4,000 years old, of course!
I Is it true that Harrods produces its own electricity?
P Yes, it does – 70% – enough for a small town. To light the outside of the building, we use 11,500 light bulbs.
I Really! Tell me, how many customers do you have on an average day, and how much do they spend?
P About 30,000 people come on an average day. But during the sales the number increases to 300,000 customers a day. How much do they spend? Well, on average, customers spend about £1.5 million a day. The record for one day is £9 million.
I £9 million in one day?
P Yes, on the first day of the January sales.
I Harrods says it sells everything, to everybody, everywhere. Is that really true?
P Oh, yes, of course. Absolutely everything…

2.3

R=Receptionist, J=James

R Good morning. Bresson Translation Services.
J Oh, hello. Could I speak to Monique Bresson, please?
R Who's calling, please?
J This is James Turner from *Wine and Dine* magazine.
R Hold the line, please, Mr Turner… I'm sorry. She's in a meeting. Can I take a message?
J Yes. Could you ask her to call me? My number is 0171 331 8579.
R 331 8579. Thank you. I'll give her your message.
J Thank you. Goodbye.

2.4

R=Receptionist, J=James, M=Monique

R Bresson Translation Services.
J Can I speak to Monique Bresson, please?
R Who's calling, please?
J It's James Turner.
R Hold the line, Mr Turner. (*phone rings*) Monique?
M Speaking.
R I have James Turner on line 2 for you…

2.5

R=Receptionist, J=James

R Good afternoon. Bresson Translation Services.
J Good afternoon. This is James Turner again. Is Ms Bresson there, please?
R I'm afraid she's in Paris this afternoon. Can I give her a message?
J Er… yes. Could you tell her that the meeting with Mr Michelmore is on Wednesday at eleven o'clock?
R Could you spell that, please?
J Yes. It's M-I-C-H-E-L-M-O-R-E. And could you ask her to call him? His number is 0171 623 4459.
R Yes, Mr Turner. I'll give her your message.
J Thank you.

UNIT 3

Language focus   p. 18

Past Simple, regular and irregular verbs

1, 2   Discussion: tourist centres.
3   Listening: a visitor describes his stay in
       the UK.   3.1 🔊
4   Gap-fill: Past Simple.
5   Listen to check.   3.2 🔊
       Grammar analysis: Past Simple.   p. 4 📖

Practice   p. 19

1   Irregular verb test.   p. 16 📖
       Pronunciation: regular past tense endings.   3.3 🔊   p. 21 📖
2   Gap-fill: postcard.
3, 4   Group survey: a visit to the UK.   3.1 RF
5   Past time expressions: question and answer.   3.2 RF
6   Writing: postcard or report.   3.3 RF
                                                            p. 18 📖

Wordpower   p. 22

Holidays and travel

1   Complete a word map.
2   Word groups.
3   Create a word map.
4   Pairwork interviews: holidays.   p. 22 📖

Skills focus   p. 23

Reading. World events, the Olympics and Expo

1   Read and discuss advertisement.
2   Articles about the Olympics and Expo: read
       and prepare questions for another group.
3   Answer questions.
4   Discussion: world events.
5   Project: prepare presentation or advertisement
       about local event or local area.

Social English   p. 25

Welcoming a visitor, topics for first meetings,
conversation strategies

1   Arriving for a meeting.   3.4 🔊
2   Suitable topics for first meetings.
3   Welcoming a visitor.   3.5 🔊
4–6   Conversation over lunch:
       conversation strategies.   3.6 🔊
7   Conversation topics: plan questions.
8   Role-play: visitor and host.   p. 18 📖   3.4 RF
                                                            p. 23 📖

Language focus **1** Prompt if necessary with questions: *What kind of places do people like to visit on holiday/tours? Inside? Outside? New? Old? For sightseeing? To see something special?*

2 Discuss answer to question. Encourage students to give full reasons. Use the pictures of Venice, Rio, Bath and Paris to stimulate discussion, if necessary.

3.1 ⏺ **3** Check vocabulary on Tourist Board Survey form.

⚠ Length of stay – *How long did you stay?*
- Focus question: *Did Massimo Reale and his wife enjoy their holiday?*
- Check students are familiar with pronunciation of *Highlands* and *Edinburgh*.
- Play tape once. Check answer to focus question.
- Play tape again. Students complete survey.
- Check answers, whole class.

⚷ Profession	engineer
Length of stay	twelve days (two-day meeting, ten days in Scotland)
Places visited	London/Edinburgh/the Scottish Highlands
Activities	sightseeing/touring/walking in the mountains

4 Students work in pairs to complete conversation. Tell them to write only the verbs they know at this stage. They can complete others as they listen.

⚷ 1 lasted   4 invited   7 didn't visit   10 ate   13 went
2 stayed   5 Did, go   8 did, do   11 didn't have   14 visited
3 did, stay   6 spent   9 saw   12 Did, visit   15 took

3.2 ⏺ **5** Play tape once, pausing for students to write/check verbs.
- Check spelling of irregular verbs.

Past Simple
- Ask students to find examples in interview 2 of: a question, a positive statement, a negative statement.
- Write students' suggestions for examples on board and focus on form: *-ed* ending of regular verbs, and *did* and *didn't* for questions and negatives. Stress the use of the infinitive with *did* and *didn't*.
- Students complete grammar rules in pairs.
- Check answers, whole class.

⚷ Use the Past Simple for finished situations and actions in the past.
To make the negative, use *did + not (didn't)+* infinitive.
To make the question, use *did +* subject *+* infinitive.
- Check short answers with prompt questions, whole class: *Did Dr Lebrun visit Scotland? Did she see Cats? Did you come to the last class? Did you...?*

Refer students to Pocket Book p. 4.

Practice **1** Students work in pairs. Make sure this is timed! (3 minutes)
- Refer students to Pocket Book p. 16 to check answers.

⚷ eat/ate   come/came   do/did   fly/flew   find/found   have/had   meet/met
say/said   see/saw   spend/spent   think/thought   take/took
Follow-up activity Students cover past tense forms and test each other in pairs.

Pronunciation **①** Focus on the /ɪd/ pronunciation of *-ed* ending with verb ending in *t* or *d*.
⚷ The *-ed* ending of *visited*, *lasted*, and *attended* is pronounced as an extra syllable, /ɪd/.

3.3 ⏺ **②** Write symbols on board and check students can hear the difference: *stayed/walked/rented.*
- Play tape once while students tick sounds.
- Play tape again, pausing for choral and individual repetition.
⚷ watched /t/   enjoyed /d/   invited /ɪd/   toured /d/   visited /ɪd/   talked /t/
attended /ɪd/

3.3 ⏺ **③** Students complete rule in pairs.
⚷ In the Past Simple, when the infinitive ends in *d* or *t*, pronounce the *-ed* ending as /ɪd/.

2 Check verbs and elicit past tense forms of verbs in box through questions: *Who did you meet yesterday? What did you visit on your last holiday?* etc.
- Students complete postcard individually. Warn them that some spaces have more than one possibility.
- Check answers, whole class.

1 came	3 did	5 rented	7 walked	9 met	11 Did, have
2 spent/had	4 visited/saw	6 toured	8 saw/visited	10 didn't understand	

3 Divide students into groups, Group A to prepare questions and Group B to work out scenario.

4 Students from Group A each interview a student from Group B.
Group A (Possible questions)

What's your name?	Did you visit any interesting places?
What do you do?	What did you do in the evenings?
Did you come to the UK on business?	Where did you stay?
How many days did you spend in London?	

 Resource file 3.1

5 Set a time limit for this activity.
- Feedback on answers. *Tell us about your partner. Tell us about a week ago.* etc.

 Resource file 3.2

6 Students can 'send' their postcard or report to another person in the class, who then asks the sender questions about his/her trip.

 Resource file 3.3

Wordpower **1** Students complete word map in pairs.
- Check answers, whole class. Check the words added.

Accommodation: hotel/holiday flat/tent/bed and breakfast/villa
Travel: plane/coach/train/ferry
Activities: (beach) sunbathing/swimming/sailing (mountains) climbing/skiing (cities) sightseeing/museums
- Draw students' attention to organization of word map: main category, sub-categories, etc.

2 Students complete phrases in pairs.
(Possible answers)

to have a	walking holiday	to go	sightseeing
	climbing holiday		skiing
to do some	swimming		windsurfing
	windsurfing		hitch-hiking
	sailing/snorkelling		

3 Students make word maps individually or as pairwork, or as homework. If an overhead projector or flip-chart is available, students can write word maps on a transparency or flip-chart sheet and present them to whole class.

4 Before interviews, tell students they will have to report back on their partner's holiday.
- Feedback, whole class.

Skills focus This advertisement presents the image of Spain as an excellent place for business, as well as for holidays, leisure, and culture. Spain hosted two major world events in 1992 – the Barcelona Olympics, and the Expo in Seville.

1 Check vocabulary in advertisement: *a conference/a convention, a network of hotels, conference facilities, the bottom line* (= *the fundamental truth, basic reality*)

 Expo (Exposition) has this special world fair use, but is not the normal word for art exhibition, etc.
- Check suggested reasons, whole class.

network of hotels with conference facilities, wonderful climate, good food and wine, museums and art galleries

2 Divide class into groups to read texts and prepare questions. Make sure they write legibly, to exchange questions with other group.

Subject questions *Who opened Expo?*

3 Students exchange questions, and refer to text for answers.
- Groups return answered questions for checking.

4 Write *Advantages* and *Disadvantages* on the board. List students' ideas under these two headings.

5 Projects can be done as group activities, and presented to the whole class.

Social English   This Social English section focuses on the importance of both sides listening carefully and asking questions, in order to 'build' a good conversation. In professional/social situations, people with a low level of competence in the target language often give only *Yes* and *No* answers, and do not ask many questions or initiate conversation. This may make it difficult to build a relationship and can give the impression that the person is passive and uninterested.

3.4 **1** Use photo to set scene: *What do you think she is saying?*
- Play tape once.
- Check answers to questions, whole class.

◎⟶ 1 He wants to see Wayne Brown.   2 She asks him to take a seat.

2 Students read through topics and decide which topics are appropriate.
- Discuss answers, whole class. If class is monolingual, ask students if they know of countries where choice of topics for first meetings is different from their own. List the differences on board. Use these examples to discuss/raise awareness of the importance of knowing such things in order not to offend or be offended in cross-cultural situations.

3.5 **3** Play tape once.
- Students check answers in pairs.
- Play tape again if necessary.
- Check answers, whole class.

◎⟶ Did you have any problems finding us?   How was your flight?

3.6 **4** Play tape once.
- Students note down answers.
- Play tape again if necessary.
- Check answers, whole class.

◎⟶ 1 He came to San Francisco as a student, and discovered Californian wines.
     2 He got a job with a wine merchant, then wrote an article for a wine magazine.

5 Students discuss points in pairs.
- Discuss answers, whole class. Stress the importance of points 1, 3, 4, and 5 for building a conversation and creating a good initial relationship.

◎⟶ 1, 3, 4, and 5 are important to make a good conversation.

3.6 **6** Play tape again.

◎⟶ James and Wayne do all these things, so their conversation is a good model.

7 Allow time for preparation of questions.
- Write questions on board, under headings given.
- Partially erase the questions one by one, leaving one-word prompts. Each time elicit question erased and those erased previously, by pointing to the prompt.

8 Before doing the role-play, students decide in their pairs who they are, which place they are visiting, and the reason for the visit.
- Monitor pairwork.

    Resource file 3.4

Tapescript Unit 3

3.1 🔊
Interview 1
I=Interviewer, M=Massimo Reale

I   So, Mr Reale, you come from Italy and you're an engineer. Did you visit the UK on business or for a holiday?

M   For both. I attended a two-day international meeting of my company at a hotel in London, then I flew to Scotland with my wife for a holiday.

I   How long did you stay there?

M   Ten days.

I   And how did you spend your time in Scotland?

M   Well, we did some sightseeing in Edinburgh. We thought it was a very beautiful city, but we didn't spend all our time there. We rented a car and toured the Scottish Highlands. We also walked in the mountains.

I   Did you stay in hotels in Scotland?

M   No, we didn't. We stayed in bed and breakfast accommodation in small villages. We met dozens of local people and we found them very friendly, but we didn't always understand them!

I   Did you enjoy your holiday?

M   Oh, yes, we had a wonderful time. We really needed more time…

3.2 🔊
Interview 2
I=Interviewer, L=Dr Lebrun

I   So, Doctor Lebrun, you came to London for a medical congress and for a holiday…

L   Yes, that's right.

I   How many days did you spend in the UK?

L   Eight days. The congress lasted three days, and after that I stayed with friends.

I   Where did you stay?

L   In a hotel for the congress, and then my friends invited me to stay in their London flat.

I   Did you go to any museums or art galleries in London?

L   Yes, I did. I spent hours in the British Museum and the National Gallery, but I didn't visit the Tate Gallery.

I   And what did you do in the evenings?

L   My friends and I saw the musical *Cats*, and we ate in some very good restaurants, but I didn't have time to go to the theatre or the opera.

I   Did you visit any places outside London?

L   Yes. We went to Bath and visited the Roman Baths and took photos of Bath's famous architecture.

3.3 🔊

stayed	invited
walked	toured
rented	visited
watched	talked
enjoyed	attended

3.4 🔊
R=Receptionist, J=James

R   Good afternoon, can I help you?

J   Good afternoon. My name's James Turner. I have an appointment with Wayne Brown.

R   Oh, yes, Mr Turner. Mr Brown is expecting you. Please take a seat and I'll tell him you're here… Mr Brown, I have Mr Turner in reception for you… OK. Mr Turner, Mr Brown will be with you in a moment.

3.5 🔊
W=Wayne, J=James

W   Hello, James! Welcome to California! It's good to meet you.

J   It's good to be here at last.

W   Did you have any problems finding us?

J   No. Jack Michelmore gave me directions in London last week. I got a taxi here.

W   Good. How was your flight?

J   There was a short delay in London, but the flight was fine. Fortunately, I slept on the plane, so I'm not very tired.

W   Glad to hear it. You've got a busy programme ahead. Let's discuss it over lunch. I booked a table for one-thirty. Do you like Mexican food?

3.6 🔊
W=Wayne, J=James

W   How did your career in the wine business begin?

J   Right here, actually. I came to San Francisco when I was a student. That was when I discovered Californian wines.

W   When was that?

J   Nearly fifteen years ago.

W   Did you work in California?

J   No. I returned to Europe, and I got a job with a wine merchant. Later, I wrote an article for a wine magazine. That's how it all began! How did you get into the wine business?

W   Well, actually, I'm a lawyer. But I grew up in Napa Valley. My uncle owns a winery.

J   Really? How big is it?

W   Its production is quite small. But the wines are excellent. Anyway, when I finished university my uncle asked me to work for him. I look after his business affairs.

UNIT 4

Language focus   p. 26

Comparative and superlative adjectives

1, 2   Discussion: exciting world cities.
3   Reading: what makes Sydney exciting.
4   Find comparative and superlative adjectives
       in text: complete chart.

       Grammar analysis: comparative and
       superlative adjectives.   p. 5 PB

Practice   p. 28

1   Gap-fill: magazine articles.   4.1 RF
       Pronunciation: stress in single words.   4.1, 4.2, 4.3 ⬛ p. 27 WB
2   Pairwork: city statistics.
3   Game: guess the city.
4   Pairwork survey: cities.
5   Writing: travel article.   4.2 RF
                                                   p. 24 WB

Wordpower   p. 30

Hotels

1   Discussion: hotel facilities.
2   Matching exercise: pictograms and
       facilities.
3   Role-play: finding out about hotel
       facilities.
4   Identifying pictures: bathroom equipment.   4.3 RF
                                                   p. 28 WB

Skills focus   p. 31

Listening. Comparisons, travel

1, 2   A consultant's presentation about holiday
       destinations: complete chart.   4.4 ⬛
3   Groupwork: discuss information; prepare
       and give presentation.
4   Project: prepare and give presentation on
       holiday recommendations.

Social English   p. 32

Staying at a hotel

1, 2   Scene-setting: booking a hotel.   4.5 ⬛
3   Arriving at a hotel.   4.6 ⬛
4, 5   Checking out of a hotel.   4.7 ⬛
6   Role-play: booking, checking in
       and checking out.   p. 19 PB   4.4 RF
                                                   p. 29 WB

1 Discuss question, whole class. Encourage students to speculate. Prompt with questions: *What makes a city exciting? Cultural attractions? Entertainment and night-life? Buildings? Geographical position? Cosmopolitan character? People? Is this city exciting? Why? Why not?*

2 Before students begin, elicit possible categories, and check vocabulary: *cultural attractions: museums, art galleries, theatres, concerts, exhibitions, places of historical interest; entertainment: restaurants, cafés, bars, clubs, night-life; leisure and sports facilities.*
  • Each group presents their list. Write features on board.
  • Agree on the five most popular features, erasing others as the class reaches consensus.

 (Possible answers)
nightlife, beaches, restaurants, museums, cinemas, theatres, good hotels, beautiful buildings, famous sights

3 Before reading, use photos to elicit/check vocabulary: *harbour, bridge, opera house, waterfront*
  • After students have read article, check vocabulary: *Sydneysiders* (= people who live in Sydney), *adventurous design, spectacular building, original estimate*
  • Whole class feedback on which features Sydney has.
excited and *exciting*

4 Give students time to complete the table in pairs.
  • Check answers, whole class. Supply missing information, if necessary.
 biggest   few   largest   nearest   older   oldest   healthier   liveliest
loveliest   most cosmopolitan   more enjoyable   most exciting   more impressive
best   more   less

Comparative and superlative adjectives
  • Students read examples and complete rules.
  • Check answers, whole class.
Two-syllable adjectives ending in -y
 To make the superlative, change the *-y* to *-i* and add *-est* to the end of the adjective.
Other two-syllable adjectives and three-syllable adjectives
 To make the superlative, put *most* before the adjective.
The biggest city in Australia, but *Australia's biggest city* (no article).

 Refer students to Pocket Book p. 5

Practice **1** Check vocabulary in first article: *wide range, crowded, suitable, accessible*
far/further. Pocket Book p. 5.
  • Students complete article individually.
  • Check answers, whole class.

1 easiest	5 most beautiful	9 most accessible	13 more peaceful
2 widest	6 most dangerous	10 best	
3 more crowded	7 safer	11 farther (further)	
4 noisier	8 more suitable	12 longer	

  • Ask questions about Sydney's beaches for further practice: *What are the advantages of Bondi Beach? And the disadvantages? Which is the best beach for children? Which is the nearest to Sydney?*
  • Check vocabulary in second article: *excursion, balloon flights*
  • Students complete article individually.
  • Check answers, whole class.

14 most popular	16 finest	18 best	20 cheaper	22 most expensive
15 oldest	17 more famous	19 fewer	21 most exciting	

  • Ask students to think of two questions about the article.
  • Ask and answer questions, whole class.
Alternative activity Divide students into pairs, AA, BB. AA prepare questions on first text, BB prepare questions on second. Then change pairs, AB, AB, and students ask each other questions.

 Resource file 4.1

② Write the adjectives in the box on board. Check the comparative and superlative forms.
  ● **Students work through chart in pairs, to make as many comparisons as they can.**
🔑 (Possible answers)
The USA is bigger than Australia.
The USA is smaller than Canada.
The population of Canberra is smaller than the population of Ottawa.
Australia has the smallest population.
Washington DC has more citizens than Canberra.
The population of Australia is lower than the population of Canada.
  ● **Ask students to make true/false statements about the countries, whole class. Elicit correction of false statements.**
  Follow-up activity Spot test. Write the words *comparative* and *superlative* on the board. Divide students into Groups A and B. Students call out an adjective in turn. Teacher points to either *comparative* or *superlative*. Students from other group give answer. Correct answers score one point. Students get an extra point if they can then make a correct sentence using the adjective.

③ Model game with example: *It's colder than Sydney. It's bigger. It's on a river, not the sea. It's older than Sydney*, etc. (answer: *London*)

④ Check vocabulary from survey form.
  ● Make sure students realize some questions are with *is*, some with *has*. Model two questions, if necessary.
  ● Feedback, whole class. Write two (or three) cities from each question from the survey on board. Ask students to give their opinions and reasons: *I think X has worse traffic jams/a more efficient public transport system/a better climate than Y because...*
  Follow-up activity Do students agree that Sydney is an exciting city? How does it compare with the city they originally chose in Language focus 1? Mini-discussion, whole class or groups.

⑤ Students can brainstorm ideas for this in pairs or small groups in class, then write the paragraph for homework.

 Resource file 4.2

Wordpower ① Write *business trip* and *family holiday* on board. Write students' suggestions on board under each category.
🔑 (Possible answers)
a. business trip: conference/meeting rooms, equipment such as computers, OHPs
b. family holiday: good food, comfortable rooms, swimming-pool, family bar

2 Students match as many items as they can individually, then check in pairs.

in-room hair-dryer 7   cocktail bar 2   restaurant 1   fitness centre 8
facilities for disabled 5   swimming-pool 4   tennis courts 10   in-room safes 9
conferences and meetings 6   air-conditioning 3

- Students cover list, and test each other using pictograms.

3 Allow time for students to absorb information or prepare questions in AA, BB pairs.
- Role-play back-to-back, AB, AB, to simulate telephone conversation.

4 After the matching activity, practise with a game: 'Ask the right question'. In pairs, students ask questions to elicit the item they are thinking of. *What's the thing you use when you...?*

8 bath   10 shower   11 tap   1 toilet   4 shaver socket   6 hair-dryer   9 towel
3 bathrobe   5 soap   7 toothbrush   2 toothpaste

 Resource file 4.3

Skills focus **1** Check vocabulary: *reward, exotic holiday*

The company's most successful sales staff.

- Ask students to suggest why the Great Barrier Reef is called 'The eighth wonder of the World'.

The Great Barrier Reef is the world's largest structure built up by living creatures – it includes thousands of living corals which are home to fish, plants, and animals. It is more than 2,000 km long, and 80 km wide, and stretches from Australia's Queensland coast to Papua New Guinea. Astronauts can see it from outer space. Today 98% of the reef is protected as the Great Barrier Reef Marine Park in order to preserve it as one of the world's greatest natural resources, perhaps even the most incredible array of life on the planet.

4.4 **2** Give students time to read chart. Check vocabulary: *travel consultant, relaxing, scuba diving, exclusive, snorkelling, tropical fish, peaceful*
- Focus question: *Which island do you think is the best one for you?* Play the presentation once.
- Play the tape again, pausing after each section to give students time to complete information.
- Students compare their answers in pairs.
- If necessary, play tape again, pausing to elicit answers as a final check.

	Hamilton	Heron	Bedarra
General information	largest island, widest choice of activities, nightlife	quieter, more relaxing than Hamilton, national park, birdwatching	smaller, more exclusive most expensive
Accommodation	for 1,400 people	for 250 people lower prices	for 32 people people only
Facilities	restaurants, bars, nightclubs, shops	1 restaurant	2 restaurants
Sport	all water sports, tennis, golf	scuba-diving, snorkelling	swimming, windsurfing, sailing, tennis

3 After they have made their decisions, groups present their choice of people and islands, and their reasons, to the other groups.

4 Groups prepare presentation in class. Set a time limit for the presentation.
- Before individuals give presentations, tell the audience to be ready to ask follow-up questions.

Social English ① Find out if students stay at hotels on professional trips. If so, who makes the hotel booking, and how? By phone, fax, letter?
- Check vocabulary: *confirm, confirmation, reserve/book, booking*
- Students read through faxes.

4.5 ⏻
- Play tape once.
- Students compare answers in pairs.
- Check answers, whole class.

⌖ 1 James wants to book another room for a colleague for 4 April.
2 The hotel is fully booked for 4 April.

4.5 ⏻ ② Play tape again. Students complete conversation.
- Check answers, whole class.

⌖ single room
I'm very sorry
what a pity
Thank you for your help

4.6 ⏻ ③ Students read through phrases, and mark who uses each phrase, hotel receptionist (h) or guest (g).
- Check students understand difference between *key* and (electronic) *keycard*.
- Practise pronunciation of phrases.
- Play tape. Students tick phrases they hear.
- Students check answers in pairs.

⌖ I have a reservation.
Could you fill in this form, please, and sign here?
Here's your key.
The porter will take your luggage.
Could I have an early morning call, at 6.30?
Do you need anything else?

4.7 ⏻ ④ Elicit phrases students know for checking out of a hotel. Prompt with questions: *You want to check out. What do you say?*
- Play tape. Students tick T or F.
- Check answers, whole class.

⌖ 1 False
2 True

4.7 ⏻ ⑤ Play tape again. Students complete conversation.

⌖ Could I have
Can I pay
we take
by credit card
you enjoyed
very much

⑥ Divide class into Student A and Student B groups. Allow them time to read through their roles for Situations 1 and 2, check the phrases they need and rehearse.
- Students A and B do role-play in pairs.
- Monitor role-play.
- Repeat preparation phase for Situations 3 and 4. Make sure students realize their role is different now.
- Students A and B do role-play in pairs.
- Monitor role-play.
- Students can change roles and do the role-play again. Monitor as previously.

 Resource file 4.4

Tapescript Unit 4

4.1

a. suitable   b. expensive

4.2

Example excitement b.
1 popular   4 impressive
2 surprising   5 exciting
3 dangerous   6 beautiful

4.3

1 producer   4 quality
2 consultant   5 translator
3 customer   6 telephone

4.4

T=Travel consultant
T   Good morning, everyone, and thank you for asking me to make this presentation. I'm going to describe three islands in Australia's Great Barrier Reef – they are Hamilton, Heron, and Bedarra. These islands offer a range of accommodation and activities suitable for the different types of people you want to send on this holiday.
First, some general information about Hamilton. It's the largest of the islands, and it has the widest choice of activities. It's the most popular island for young people and has a lively nightlife. It offers more accommodation than the other two islands – there's accommodation for 1,400 people. Prices are high. It has more facilities than the two other islands – lots of restaurants, bars, nightclubs, and shops. It also has the best choice of sporting activities – all the water sports, as well as tennis and golf. So, Hamilton is the biggest and liveliest island, and it offers the most activities.
The second island, Heron, is quieter and more relaxing than Hamilton. It's a national park, and it's a wonderful place for anyone interested in bird-watching. There is accommodation for 250 people, and prices here are lower than on Hamilton. It has only one restaurant and there are no bars or nightclubs. For people who are interested in scuba-diving and snorkelling this island is more exciting than the others because Heron is actually part of the Great Barrier Reef, so when you swim around Heron, you see the thousands of different kinds of tropical fish that make the Great Barrier Reef so famous. So, this island is smaller than Hamilton and is suitable for people who want a quiet place where they can enjoy the wildlife.
The third island, Bedarra, is a lot smaller and more exclusive than the other two islands. People also say it's also the most beautiful. It's an ideal place for people who want to escape noise… and it's even more peaceful than Heron because they don't allow children under 16 years old on Bedarra. There is accommodation for 32 people only, in luxury villas. It's the most expensive island of the three. There are two restaurants which serve very good food and there's a good choice of sporting activities – swimming, wind-surfing, sailing, and tennis. So, to sum up, Bedarra is the smallest, quietest, and most exclusive island of the three.

4.5

R=Receptionist, J=James
R   Hotel Leon d'Oro. Buongiorno.
J   Buongiorno. Do you speak English?
R   Yes. How can I help you?
J   My name is James Turner. Last week I booked a room from the 3rd to the 6th of April… er, you confirmed the reservation by fax.
R   Oh, yes, Mr Turner. I remember.
J   I'd like to book a single room, for a colleague, for the 4th of April.
R   Let me see. Oh, I'm very sorry, Mr Turner, but we're fully booked on the 4th of April, because of Vinitaly, you see.
J   Oh, what a pity.
R   You could try the other hotels in Verona.
J   Yes, I'll do that. Thank you for your help. Goodbye.
R   We look forward to seeing you on the 3rd of April, Mr Turner. Goodbye.

4.6

J   Good evening. My name is Turner. I have a reservation.
R   Yes, a single room for four nights?
J   Yes, that's right.
R   Could you fill in this form, please, and sign here? Thank you. Here's your key. Your room is on the first floor. The porter will take your luggage.
J   Thank you. Oh, could I have an early morning call, at 6.30?
R   Yes, certainly. Do you need anything else?
J   No, that's all, thank you.

4.7

J   Could I have my bill, please? Can I pay by credit card or eurocheque?
R   Yes, we take both.
J   I'll pay by credit card, then.
R   That's fine. I hope you enjoyed your stay here.
J   Oh, yes, very much. And I'm sure I'll be back here next April, for Vinitaly.
R   We'll be delighted to see you again, Mr Turner. Goodbye, and have a good trip back.
J   Thank you. Goodbye.

UNIT 5

Language focus   p. 38

Mass and count nouns, *some/any*, *a lot of/much/many*

1	Discussion: problems of flying.	
2	Reading: leaflet giving advice on healthy flying.	
3, 4	Listening: describing a flight.	5.1 ▢
	Grammar analysis: Mass and count nouns.	p. 6 PB
	some/any,	p. 6 PB
	a lot of/much/many.	p. 6 PB

Practice   p. 41

1	*some/any*. Sentence completion.	
2	*a lot of/much/many*. Gap-fill: postcard.	5.1 RF
	Pronunciation: 'schwa' in single words. 5.2, 5.3 ▢	p. 33 WB
3, 4	Pairwork survey: how you spend your time.	
5	Compare lifestyles.	p. 30 WB

Wordpower   p. 42

Food vocabulary

1, 2	Classification: types of food.	
3, 4	Methods of cooking.	
5	Game: guess the dish.	
6	Prepare a menu.	5.2 RF
		p. 33 WB

Skills focus   p. 43

Reading. Diet and health

1	Magazine article about healthy diet: find answers to questions.	
2	Discussion: diet and health.	5.3 RF
3	Project: prepare short talk on national cuisines, *or* compile and present a healthy menu.	

Social English   p. 44

At a restaurant: recommending, ordering, offering

1–4	At a restaurant.	5.4, 5.5, 5.6 ▢
5	Complete conversation.	
6	Role-play: guest and host/hostess.	
7	Role-play: in a restaurant.	p. 19 PB p. 35 WB

① Discuss questions with whole class.

⊙⊸ (Possible answers)

People often feel stiff, suffer from jet-lag, tiredness, and headaches after long flights. They can do exercises to reduce tiredness and stiffness during flight. They can try to sleep. They can be careful of what they eat and drink.

② Before reading, look at the pictures and diagrams. Encourage students to speculate on the purpose of the *Well-being Kit*, exercises, etc.
  - Check vocabulary: *jet-lag, tired/tiredness, stiff/stiffness, bad effects, fatty foods*
  - Students read text individually.
  - Students discuss answers in pairs.
  - Check answers, whole class.

⊙⊸ The programme suggests that travellers don't drink alcohol, tea, or coffee as these can increase jet-lag. They suggest water or juices are better. There is a special menu with light meals. The programme also gives detailed exercises for passengers to prevent stiffness.

5.1 🔲 **③** Check vocabulary: *it (really) works (= is effective)*
  - Give students time to read T/F statements.
  - Play tape. Students note T or F.
  - Check answers, whole class.

⊙⊸ 1 F   2 T   3 F   4 T   5 F

5.1 🔲 **④** Look at example and check students understand task.
  - Play tape again. Students underline correct alternative.
  - Students check answers in pairs.

⊙⊸ 1 didn't have any   3 didn't drink any   5 some   7 drank a lot of
    2 a lot of   4 any   6 Not many

  - If necessary, play tape again for final check.

Mass and count nouns
  - Check students understand the terms *mass* and *count*. Refer to the examples in the lists, and elicit difference. If necessary, draw a blob (mass) and sticks (count) on board to illustrate.
  - Students complete mass and count lists individually.
  - Check lists, whole class.

⊙⊸ **Mass**   *coffee   information   alcohol   sleep   champagne   *fruit juice
              advice   luggage

Count *coffee   magazine   *fruit juice   trip   plane   problem   passenger
              vegetable

  - Students complete grammar rules in pairs.
  - Check answers, whole class.

⊙⊸ Mass nouns do not have a plural form. We cannot count them.
Some *nouns are both mass and count.

  - To explain nouns that are both mass and count, write these examples on the board:
1 a. I try to get some <u>exercise</u> every day.
    b. I tried to do some <u>exercises</u> on the plane.
2 a. I like to spend <u>time</u> with my children in the evenings.
    b. I see my parents three or four <u>times</u> a month.
3 a. We import <u>coffee</u> from Brazil.
    b. Can I have a <u>coffee</u>, please?
    Elicit/explain:
1a. = general activity. 1b. = different, specific exercises
2a. = 'clock' time. 2b. = gives frequency, answers *How often...?*
3a. = coffee, the product. 3b. = a cup of coffee.

Refer students to Pocket Book p. 6

some and *any*

Use of *some* in questions that are offers or requests.
- Students read examples and complete grammar rules in pairs.
- Check answers, whole class.

Use *any* in negative sentences, and for questions.
Use *some* and *any* with both mass and count nouns.
- You may want to go straight to Practice 1 to give a change of focus at this point.

a lot of/much/many

- Students read examples and complete grammar rules in pairs.
- Check answers, whole class.

Use *a lot of* with both mass and count nouns in positive sentences.
Use *much* with mass nouns in negative sentences and in questions.
Use *many* with count nouns in negative sentences and in questions.

Refer students to Pocket Book, p. 6.

Practice ❶ Students complete sentences individually.
- Students check answers in pairs.

1 some	3 some	5 some	7 any	9 any
2 any	4 any	6 some	8 some	10 some

❷ Students complete letter individually.
- Check answers, whole class.

1 a lot of	3 many	5 a lot of	7 a lot of
2 much	4 a lot of	6 many	8 many

Resource file 5.1

Pronunciation ① Play tape once. Students repeat words.
5.2 🔊   • Point out that 'schwa' (/ə/) is used in the unstressed syllables. Ask students which syllables have the main stress.

5.3 🔊 ② Play tape. Students mark main stress.

5.3 🔊 ③ Play tape again. Students underline syllables with 'schwa'.
- Check answers, whole class.

1 magazine	3 exercise	5 problem	7 vegetable
2 passenger	4 advice	6 cigarette	8 brochure

④ Students repeat words.
- Point out that 'schwa' is the most common sound in English, and occurs in unstressed syllables.

---

❸ Check example questions. Draw students' attention to *How much* (*time*), *How many* (*hours*), *spend time on*.
- Students fill in first column individually.
- Students prepare questions in AA, BB pairs.

❹ Each student interviews a student from another pair, AB, AB.

❺ Compile feedback from interviews on board, whole class.
- Compare lifestyles. *Who spends most time…*
Follow-up activity Discussion on how to improve time management. Elicit general suggestions.

Wordpower ❶ Before the pairwork, check the menu categories. Prompt with questions: *Do you know the name of a starter? A main course? A dessert?*
- Tell pairs to write the foods they know under the correct headings.
- Monitor pairwork. Make a note of vocabulary which is new to any students and write it on board, under relevant headings.
- Check meaning of vocabulary on board.
- Give students time to complete food vocabulary lists.

- Check lists, and practise pronunciation, whole class. Add word stress marks, where appropriate.

Meat	**Poultry**	**Fish/Seafood**	**Vegetables**	**Fruit**
pork	chicken	prawns	mushrooms	lemon
veal		trout	potatoes	strawberries
		Dover sole	onions	bananas
			green beans	figs
				passion fruit

2 Give students time to think of other foods.
- List students' suggestions on board.

3 Students underline examples individually.

smoked   grilled   roast   sautéed   grilled   fried

4 Students match pictures.
- Check answers, whole class.

1 grilled   2 fried   3 roast

5 Check vocabulary: *ingredients*
- Ask for suggestions for other possible questions, whole class.
- Before dividing class into groups, model an example of the game yourself.

6 Check vocabulary: *vegetarian*
- Divide class into groups.
- Monitor group preparation.
- Groups present their menu.

Resource file 5.2

Skills focus 1 Before students read text, compare their answers to the questions and the reasons for their opinions.
- Students read text and check information.
- Check answers and vocabulary, whole class.

1 c. France   2 It reduces the risk of heart attack.   3 beef
4 a. France b. Spain c. Italy d. Greece. They are all made with garlic.

aioli = garlic mayonnaise (French), *gambas al ajillo* = prawns with garlic (Spanish), *bruschetta* = toasted garlic bread (Italian), *tzatziki* = yoghurt with garlic and cucumber (Greek).

2 Divide class into discussion groups.
- Nominate students to chair the discussion, preferably a different student for each topic.
- Groups report back to the whole class.

Resource file 5.3

3 If individuals choose the first project, agree a time limit for their talk before they begin to prepare.

Social English 1 Elicit phrases students know for recommending and ordering food.
Prompt with questions: *You're in a restaurant. What do you say if you want to order something? If you want to recommend?*
- Give students time to read menu (p. 42) and wine list (this page).

5.4
- Play tape once.
- Students check answers in pairs.

King prawns, smoked salmon, Dover sole, Normandy pork, a bottle of Sancerre.

5.5 **2** Play tape once.
- Encourage students to speculate, and give reasons for their opinions.

Monique.

5.6 📼 ❸ **Play tape once. Encourage students to speculate.**

🔑 (Possible answer)

Perhaps James wants to ask Monique out for dinner to celebrate *her* birthday.

5.4, 5.5, 5.6 📼 ❹ **Give students time to read through phrases.**
- **Practise pronunciation.**
- **Play all three conversations. Students tick phrases.**
- **Students check answers in pairs.**

🔑 **Recommending**

What do you recommend?

The ... is usually excellent here.

I recommend...

Ordering

I'll have...

I'd like...

Offering

Do have some more...

How about...?

Would you like...?

Accepting

Yes. That would be very nice.

Declining

Thank you, but I couldn't eat any more.

Thanking and responding

Thank you for a lovely evening.

Don't mention it.

I enjoyed it very much, too.

❺ **Students work individually to complete conversation, using list of phrases.**
- **Check answers, whole class.**

🔑 (Possible answers)

do you recommend?

duck pâté

what about veal cutlets?

that would be nice

what would you like

Red wine

I'd like that

how about

I couldn't eat any more

Are you

What about

Yes, I'd like that

for a really excellent meal

Don't mention it
- **Practise pronunciation of conversation.**
- **Students read dialogue in pairs. Then change roles.**

❻ **Give students time to plan what they will say before they begin the conversation, but encourage them not to write anything.**

❼ **Divide students into groups. Students choose their roles.**
- **Give students time to prepare their role.**
- **Monitor role-play.**
- **Students can do role-play once or twice more, changing roles.**

Tapescript Unit 5

5.1 ▶

M=Martyn, A=Ann

M Hi, Ann. Welcome back! How was your trip to the States?

A Very busy. I had a lot of meetings and, of course, I didn't have much time to see New York.

M What a pity! Actually, I have a trip there myself next week.

A Do you? Then take my advice. Do the *Well-being in the air* programme. It really works.

M Oh, I read about that in a magazine. You say it works?

A Yes. I did the programme on the flight to the States, and when I arrived in New York I didn't have any problems, no jet-lag at all. On the way back I didn't do it and I felt terrible.

M You're joking!

A Not at all. It really made a lot of difference.

M Hmm… So what did you do?

A Well, I didn't drink any alcohol or coffee, and I didn't eat any meat or rich food. I drank a lot of water and fruit juice, and I ate the meals on the *Well-being* menu. They're lighter – they have fish, vegetables, and pasta, for example. And I did some of the exercises in the programme.

M Exercises? On a plane?

A Yes. I didn't do many, of course. There isn't much space on a plane.

M How many passengers did the exercises?

A Not many!

M And how much champagne did they drink?

A A lot! It was more popular than mineral water!

M So, basically it's a choice – mineral water and exercises or champagne and jet-lag?

A That's right. It's a difficult choice!

5.2 ▶

alcohol   information   lemon

5.3 ▶

Example   potato
1 magazine   3 exercise
2 passenger   4 advice

5 problem   7 vegetable
6 cigarette   8 brochure

5.4 ▶

W=Waiter, M=Monique, J=James

W Good evening.

M Good evening. I booked a table for two. The name is Bresson.

W Oh, yes, madam. Your table is over here.

J This is a wonderful surprise, Monique. How did you know it was my birthday?

M Oh, that's a secret. Anyway, I would like to discuss the trip to Hungary with you. You need an interpreter?

J Yes, I do.

M Well, let's order first.

J It's a difficult choice. What do you recommend?

M Well, the fish is usually excellent here. Let's see. I recommend the Dover sole, or if you prefer meat, the Normandy pork.

W Are you ready to order?

M James?

J Yes, I'll have king prawns as starter, and then grilled Dover sole.

M And I'd like smoked salmon and the Normandy pork.

W Certainly, madam. And what would you like to drink?

M You choose.

J OK. A bottle of Sancerre, please.

5.5 ▶

M This wine is very good, isn't it? Do have some more, James.

J Yes, it's very good, and the fish is delicious.

M Good. I'm pleased you like it. Now, how about a dessert?

J I'm sure they're all wonderful, Monique. Thank you, but I couldn't eat any more.

M Are you sure? Would you like some coffee, then?

J Yes. That would be very nice.

M Now, about the trip to Hungary…

5.6 ▶

J Thank you for a lovely evening, Monique. I really enjoyed it.

M Don't mention it. I enjoyed it very much, too, James.

J Now. When's *your* birthday?

UNIT 6

————————————————————— Notes —————————

Language focus   p. 46

Past Simple and Present Perfect Simple, *ever*

1   Discussion: job advertisement.
2   Reading: a CV and letter of application.
3   Identify different tenses in text.
    Grammar analysis 1: Past Simple, Present   p. 7 [PB]
    Perfect Simple.
4   Listening: a job interview.   6.1 [cassette]
    Grammar analysis 2: Present Perfect Simple p. 7 [PB]
    questions, *ever*.

Practice   p. 50

1   Irregular verb test.   p. 16 [PB]
2   Pairwork: interviews.   6.1 [RF]
3   Gap-fill: biographical details.
    Pronunciation: strong and weak forms
    of *have* and *has*.   6.2, 6.3 [cassette]
4   Pairwork: job interview.
5, 6 Compare candidates for a job.
7   Writing: memo describing choice of   6.2, 6.3 [RF]
    candidates.   p. 36 [WB]

Wordpower   p. 52

Recruitment

1   Complete a word map.
2   Gap-fill: job recruitment procedures.
3   Word families.
4   Discussion: how job vacancies are filled.
5   Pairwork: discussion about recruitment.   p. 39 [WB]

Skills focus   p. 53

Listening. Interview techniques and guidelines

1   Discussion: interview techniques.
2   A consultant gives advice on attending
    an interview: complete guidelines.   6.4 [cassette]
3   Discussion: advice for candidates.
4   Compile guidelines for interviewer.   6.4 [RF]
5   Writing: a CV.
6   Project: recruiting a new employee.

Social English   p. 54

Making and changing arrangements

1   Scene-setting.
2, 3 Telephoning: making an appointment.   6.5 [cassette]
4, 5 Telephoning: changing an appointment.   6.6 [cassette]
6–9 Complete conversations: practice.
10 Role-play: making and changing   p. 20 [PB]   6.5 [RF]
    appointments.   p. 41 [WB]

Overview 6   page 38

Language focus **1** Ask students to read headline and first paragraph of job advert only.

- Check vocabulary and practise pronunciation: *exclusive facilities, corporate entertainment*
- Ask for suggestions of the personal qualities which might be needed. Prompt if necessary: *What kind of person do they want?*
- Check vocabulary: *to market, corporate travel industry, interpersonal skills*
- Students look at questions and read rest of advert.
- Students answer/discuss questions, whole class.

⊙⟶ 1 The Manager must meet and socialize with a lot of people, and make presentations.

2 Elicit components of a CV: *personal details, qualifications, professional experience*

- Check vocabulary: *corporate/business clients, conference facilities, promotional video*
- Students work in pairs to match the letter extracts to the jobs in the CV.

⊙⟶ Extract 1 = 1987 (Diploma)
Extract 2 = 1987–89 (Assistant Manager)
Extract 3 = 1990–93 (Manager)
Extract 4 = 1993–Present (Corporate Client Services Manager)

- Practise Past Simple. Ask prompt questions about Erwin Verhoot's previous jobs: *Where did he study? What happened in 1987? What did he do from 1987 to 1989?* etc.

3 Students read through letter extracts and underline verbs, individually.

- Check answers, whole class.

⊙⟶ Erwin uses the Past Simple to talk about his previous jobs. Those jobs are finished. He uses a *different* tense (Present Perfect Simple) to talk about his current job. This job is not finished.

Past Simple and Present Perfect Simple

- Students read examples and complete rules in pairs.
- Check answers, whole class.

⊙⟶ To make the Present Perfect Simple, use *has* or *have* + the past participle of the verb (*travelled, been, increased*).
Use the Past Simple for finished situations and actions in the past.
Use the Present Perfect Simple for past actions with present results.

Refer students to Pocket Book p. 7

Follow-up activities Ask students to find one example from text to match each timeline. Check possibilities, whole class.
Or Ask students to draw their own timeline. Mark one thing which is finished, and one thing in a period up to the present. Whole class feedback.

6.1 ▭ **4** Students read Olivia Lonro's CV. Check vocabulary: *cruise, consultant, corporate entertainment*

- Students read notes and questions on interviewer's notepad.
- Play tape once.
- Students note information as they listen.
- Play tape again, if necessary.
- Check answers, whole class.

⊙⟶ 1 For Europe and Japan.
2 Yes, she spent a month there in 1993.
3 Yes, a lot.
4 No.

Present Perfect Simple questions, *ever*
- Give students time to read examples and answer questions in pairs.
- Check answers, whole class.

 1 The question is made with *has* or *have* + subject + past participle.

2 *She's gone to Japan* = she's in Japan now, or on her way. *She's been to Japan* = her visit is over.

3 *ever*

- Practise pronunciation of statements with contracted *have/has*: *I've travelled a lot. She's been to Japan.* etc.

Refer students to Pocket Book p. 7

Follow-up activities Draw timelines on board. Play 6.1 again, pausing the tape after each verb. Ask students to match use to timeline.

Or Draw timelines on board. Give pairs 2 minutes to come up with one example of their own for each category. Whole class feedback.

Practice ❶ Students do test individually or in pairs. Make sure this is timed! (3 minutes).
- Students check answers in Pocket Book p. 16.

Past Simple	Past Participle
bought	bought
did	done
ate	eaten
gave	given
went	gone/been
made	made
met	met
read	read
saw	seen
wrote	written

❷ Before the interviews, ask students to underline the time expressions. Elicit other possibilities with *in the last* (*two weeks/few days*, etc.), and encourage students to use those in their additional questions.
- Practise pronunciation of short answers: *Yes, I have, No I haven't.*
- After interviews, ask students to report back on three things their partner has done.

Student A
1 Have you had a holiday this year?
2 Have you bought anything expensive recently?
3 Have you made any business trips in the last three months?
4 Have you done any sport this week?
5 Have you met any foreigners this month?

Student B
1 Have you eaten any foreign food recently?
2 Have you written any letters this week?
3 Have you had a birthday in the last six months?
4 Have you seen any good films this month?
5 Have you read any good books recently?

 Resource file 6.1

❸ Students complete extract individually. Draw attention to the time expressions (*in 1993*, *this year*, etc.) which determine use of Past Simple or Present Perfect. Refer back to timelines if necessary.
- Check answers, whole class.

1 has travelled   3 has visited   5 met   7 has produced   9 travelled
2 has made   4 spent   6 has given   8 has never travelled   10 was

Pronunciation
6.2 🔲
6.3 🔲

① Play tape twice. Ask students to repeat sentences.

② Play tape. Students mark whether they hear sound a. or b.
● Play tape again, pausing after each sentence to check answers.
🔑 1 a.   2 b.   3 b.   4 a.   5 a.   6 a.   7 b.   8 b.

③ Students can work in AA, BB pairs to prepare questions.
● After they have prepared questions, allow some time for individuals to say questions quietly to themselves.

④ Students ask and answer questions in AB pairs.

❹ Elicit suggestions of more questions for detail. Prompt with question words if necessary: *What...? How long...?*
Question 6 *been* not *gone*. Refer students again to Pocket Book p. 7, if necessary. If necessary, draw diagram: one-way ticket [→] (*gone*), return ticket [⇄] (*been*).
🔑 1 Have you (ever) worked in the tourist industry?
2 Have you (ever) done any marketing or sales?
3 Have you (ever) given any presentations?
4 Have you (ever) studied any European languages?
5 Have you (ever) travelled on a luxury train?
6 Have you (ever) been on a cruise?
7 Have you (ever) organized a conference or other corporate activity?
8 Have you (ever) wanted to work in the luxury travel industry?

❺ Give students time to think of their reasons for suggesting that their partner is suitable for the job or not. Encourage partners to say if they agree or disagree with the assessment.

❻ Divide students into groups.
● Suggest groups refer back to job advert, and draw up list of criteria, before looking at CVs.
● Monitor group work.

❼ Students can write the memo in groups, or in pairs, to give more intensive practice.
● Monitor writing of memos.
Follow-up activity Each group takes on the role of the parent company, *Travel Enterprises*, and 'receives' another group's memo. They discuss the group's choice of candidate and reasons for the choice, described in the memo. They give oral feedback of their opinion.

 Resource file 6.2, 6.3

Wordpower ❶ When students have completed word map in pairs, check answers, whole class.
🔑 Job advertisement: job title, salary, working conditions. CV: personal details, experience, qualifications. Shortlist: interview, candidate.
● Test new vocabulary from word map by asking prompt questions: *'Marketing Director' is Olivia Lonro's...?, A business degree and a diploma in hotel management are...?*
● In preparation for 2, focus on completed word map and ask students to describe how a company fills a job vacancy. Prompt with questions: *What's the first stage? What happens next?*

❷ Students complete text individually.
🔑 ● Check answers, whole class.

1 job vacancy	6 working conditions	11 experience
2 advertisement	7 career prospects	12 short list
3 job title	8 application	13 interview
4 job requirements	9 curriculum vitae	14 candidate
5 salary	10 personal details	15 appointment

3 Students complete table in pairs.
- Check answers, whole class.

Verb	Activity	Person 1	Person 2
employ	employment	employer	employee
interview	interview	interviewer	interviewee
train	training	trainer	trainee

- Check with questions: *Was Olivia the interviewer? Am I an employer or employee? Who is the trainer here? Who is the trainee?*

4 With classes of the same nationality, encourage students to talk about any differences they know about in other companies/countries.

5 Pairs prepare questions to find out how someone got a job: *Did you see an advertisement? Where?* etc.
- Students change partners and interview each other. Report back, whole class.

Skills focus **1** Divide class into groups. When they have had a little time to think of ideas, suggest they prioritize them.
- Groups present their ideas to class.
- List suggested ideas on board.

6.4 **2** Give students time to read the incomplete list of guidelines. Ask students to predict the missing information.
- Check vocabulary: *checklist, smart (-ly dressed)*
- Play tape once.
- Ask students briefly to compare the careers officer's guidelines with their original lists.
- Play tape again. Students complete guidelines.
- Students compare answers in pairs.
- Check answers, whole class.

2 Find out about the interviewer or interviewers.
3 Make a checklist of questions to ask at interview.
5 Arrive in good time.
6 Create a good first impression.
8 Don't give only 'Yes' or 'No' answers.
9 Ask questions.
10 Learn from the interview.

3 Students discuss questions in groups, then report back on their ideas to whole class.

4 Groups could present their guidelines to the class orally, or prepare a handout.

 Resource file 6.4

5 When students have finished writing, find out what extra information they have given.

6 The project can be expanded. Groups can prepare advertisements for the job they have chosen, and 'interview' members of different groups.

Social English **1** Remind students of Duncan Ross from Unit 1. (Editor and publisher of *Wine and Dine* magazine.)
- Give students time to read letter.
- Check answer to question, whole class.

(Possible answer)
Duncan is writing to invite Monique to lunch to discuss business with her.

6.5 **2** Play tape. Students write appointment in Monique's diary. Check answer, whole class.

Lunch with Duncan Ross, Tuesday, 1.30 p.m. at Claret's restaurant.

6.5 🎧 **3** Give students time to read through phrases for *Making an appointment, Saying 'yes'*, and *Saying 'no'*.
- Practise pronunciation.
- Play tape again. Students tick the phrases they hear.

🔑 **Making an appointment**
When would be convenient for you?
Is … possible for you?
Shall we say...
What time would suit you?
How about...?

Saying 'yes'
Yes, that's fine.
I look forward to meeting you...

6.6 🎧 **4** Play tape. Students note answers.
- Check answers, whole class.

🔑 1 She can't come to the meeting on Tuesday.
2 No, he has another appointment then.
3 Friday 18th.
- Read and practise pronunciation of phrases for *Changing an appointment*.

6.6 🎧 **5** Play tape again, pausing for students to tick the phrases they hear. Point out that these will be from all the groups in 3.
- Check answers, whole class.

🔑 **Making an appointment**
When are you free?
Is ... possible for you?
What about...?
Saying 'yes'
Yes, I can make it on...
See you on...

Saying 'no'
No, I'm afraid I've got another appointment then.
Changing an appointment
I'm very sorry.
I'm afraid I can't manage our meeting on...
Could we arrange another time?

6 Students work individually to complete conversation, referring to list in 3 if necessary.
- Pairs compare versions, then read conversation.

🔑 (Possible answers)

Chris	How about	that suits me fine
Andrew	I'm afraid I'm busy	Shall we say
What time would be convenient	What about	Yes, that's fine

7 Ask students to note down three appointments they have for next week on Tuesday, Wednesday, Thursday or Friday, either in the morning or the afternoon.
- Student A begins, and pairs arrange an appointment for one of those days.
- Students change partners.
- Student B begins, and pairs arrange an appointment for one of those days.

8 Follow same procedure as in 6.

🔑 (Possible answers)

Jan	are you free
speaking	Monday convenient
Armand	I'm afraid I have another appointment then
I have to cancel our meeting on Saturday	Tuesday
arrange another time	that's fine
that's fine	See you on Tuesday at 9 a.m.

9 Students change appointments made in 7.

10 Change pairs for this activity. Students can sit back-to-back for the telephone conversation.
Follow-up activity Give students five minutes to make appointments with as many people as possible. They should aim to fill their diaries.
- Ask them to change and rearrange at least three of the appointments they have made.

 Resource file 6.5

Tapescript Unit 6

6.1

I=Interviewer, O=Olivia Lonro

I Could you tell me more about your first job, with Hotel Marketing Concepts?

O Yes, certainly. I was a marketing consultant, responsible for marketing ten UK hotels. They were all luxury hotels, in the leisure sector, all of a very high standard.

I Which markets were you responsible for?

O For Europe and Japan.

I I see from your CV that you speak Japanese. Have you ever been to Japan?

O Yes, I have. I spent a month in Japan in 1993. I met all the key people in the tourist industry – the big tour operators and the tourist organizations. As I speak Japanese, I had a very big advantage…

I Yes, of course. Have you had any contact with Japan in your present job?

O Yes, I've had a lot. Cruises have become very popular with the Japanese, both for holidays and for business conferences. In fact, the market for all types of luxury holidays for the Japanese has increased a lot recently.

I Really? I'm interested to hear more about that, but first, tell me, have you ever travelled on a luxury train, the Orient Express, for example?

O No, I haven't. But I've travelled on the Glacier Express through Switzerland, and I travelled across China by train about eight years ago. I love train travel. That's why I'm very interested in this job…

6.2

a. I don't think I have.

b. Have you heard this before?

a. He hasn't arrived.

b. Robert has forgotten.

6.3

1 I think he has.

2 Have you seen him today?

3 The invoice has arrived.

4 She hasn't been here today.

5 I haven't read the instructions.

6 Yes, I have.

7 Many people have said that.

8 Inflation has gone down this year.

6.4

C=Careers officer

C What makes a good interview? First, good preparation before the interview. Prepare yourself by following three simple guidelines. Guideline number one is – find out as much as possible about the company. For example, you can get a lot of useful information from the company's brochures, annual reports, catalogues, that sort of thing. Two, find out if the interview is with one person or with a group of people, and what their jobs are. It's very useful to know something about the interviewers before you meet them. And three, make a checklist of the questions you want to ask at the interview.

Remember an interview is a two-way process. The company finds out as much as possible about you, and you find out as much as possible about the company.

So, that's what you need to do before the interview. Now, the interview itself. There are seven more guidelines to remember here. Guideline number four, dress smartly. A suit or something formal is best. Five, arrive in good time. Arriving late for the interview is the worst thing you can do. Rule number six, create a good first impression. Remember, first impressions are very important. Start the interview with a smile, a firm handshake, and a friendly manner.

Guideline number seven? Try to stay positive and relaxed during the interview. I know that's difficult. People don't usually feel relaxed during an interview, but remember, your body language gives the interviewer a lot of information about you. You want that information to be positive, not negative. Number eight – don't give only 'Yes' or 'No' answers. Talk freely about yourself, give reasons for your opinions, and explain why you're interested in the job. Nine – ask questions. Remember the check-list of questions you prepared before the interview. Show you're interested! Finally, guideline number ten: learn from the interview. Analyse your performance afterwards and think how you can improve the next time!

6.5

R=Receptionist, M=Monique, D=Duncan

R Monique, I have a Mr Duncan Ross on the line.

M Oh, yes, put him through… Hello, Mr Ross. Thank you for your letter. I'd be very interested to meet you and discuss the new project…

D That's very good news. Oh, please call me Duncan, by the way. When would be convenient for you?

M Let me see… I'm rather busy this week… Is next week possible for you? I'm free on Tuesday… or Friday, if you prefer?

D No, Tuesday suits me fine. Shall we say lunch on Tuesday, then?

M Yes, that's fine. What time would suit you?

D How about one thirty at Claret's restaurant?

M Oh, that'll be very nice.

D Good. Well, I look forward to meeting you again, Monique.

M It'll be very nice to see you again, too, Duncan. Goodbye.

6.6

M=Monique, D=Duncan

M Hello. Is that Duncan Ross?

D Yes, speaking.

M Oh, hello, Duncan. It's Monique Bresson here. I'm very sorry. I'm afraid I can't manage our meeting on Tuesday. I have to go to Rome on that day. Could we arrange another time?

D Oh, what a pity. But yes, of course. When are you free?

M Is Thursday the 17th possible for you?

D No, I'm afraid I've got another appointment then. What about Friday the 18th?

M Yes, I can make it on Friday.

D Very good. So, the same time and place? One thirty, at Claret's?

M Yes. Thank you, Duncan. And I do apologize.

D Don't mention it. It's no problem at all. Have a good trip to Rome. See you on Friday…

UNIT 7

Language focus   p. 56

Present Perfect Simple and Continuous

1	Discussion: fashion design.
2	Listening: a fashion designer describes her career. 7.1
3	Identify verb forms in tapescript.
	Grammar analysis 1: Present Perfect p. 8 PB Simple and Continuous.

Practice   p. 57

1	Identify correct verb form.
	Grammar analysis 2: *since* and *for*.
2	Complete expressions with *since* or *for*.
3	Gap-fill: magazine article. 7.1, 7.2 RF
4	Pairwork: interviews about possessions. Pronunciation: intonation of echo questions to show polite interest. 7.2, 7.3, 7.4 p. 45 WB
5	Pairwork: prepare questions for a headhunter interview.
6	Role-play: interview. p. 42 WB

Wordpower   p. 60

Describing past trends

1	Matching exercise: verbs and graphs.
2	Complete table: related verbs and nouns.
3	Adjectives/adverbs to describe trends.
4	Gap-fill: prepositions.
5	Gap-fill: description of graph.
6	Writing: describe trends. p. 46 WB

Skills focus   p. 62

Reading. Fashion industry, imports and exports

1	Article about Italian fashion industry: answer questions.
2	Complete chart with information from text and diagrams.
3	Discussion: fashion.
4	Project: prepare and give presentation: facts and figures.

Social English   p. 64

Opinions and suggestions, agreeing and disagreeing

1–4	Planning a celebration. 7.5, 7.6
5	Matching exercise: suggestions.
6	Discussion: agreeing and disagreeing.
7	Discussion: suggestions. p. 20 PB 7.3, 7.4 RF p. 47 WB

① Look at pictures. Check vocabulary: *shoes, handbag, suit, raincoat, silk scarf*
  ● Elicit names of designers students know, and likes/dislikes.
  ● Discuss answer to question, whole class. Encourage students to say which design they like most/least, and to give reasons for their opinion.
  Picture 1: Burberry's, Picture 2: Armani, Picture 3: Yves Saint Laurent

7.1 **②** Check vocabulary: *freelance, leather goods*
  ● Give students time to read headings.
  ● Play tape once.
  ● In pairs, students discuss the information they remember.
  ● Play tape again. Students complete information as they listen.
  ● Check answers, whole class.
  British
  Florence/Italy
  designer
  designer for Ferragamo
  freelance designer
  It's easier and more interesting to work as a designer in Italy.

③ Ask students to sort the verbs into different forms after they have underlined them.
  The tenses are the Present Simple, Past Simple, the Present Perfect Simple, and the Present Perfect Continuous.

Present Perfect Simple and Present Perfect Continuous
  ● Students read examples and complete rule for Present Perfect Simple.
  ● Check answer, whole class.
  Use the Present Perfect Simple for past actions in a time period up to the present when we give the quantity.
  ● Ask students to think of their own true examples. Model with sentences about yourself: *I've been a teacher since..., I've given ... lessons this week.* As this use of the Present Perfect is difficult for students whose first language uses another Present tense for situations and actions beginning in the past and continuing to the present, stress the fact that we do not use the Present Simple or Present Continuous tense here in English, but the Present Perfect.
  ● Students read examples and complete rules for Present Perfect Continuous.
  To make the Present Perfect Continuous, use *has/have* + *been* + *-ing* form of the verb. Use the Present Perfect Continuous for an action that began in the past and continues to the present.
  ● Draw attention to timeline. Ask students to think of their own true examples.
 have been living and *have lived*. Often there is little difference in meaning. The Continuous is more usual.
  ● Draw students' attention to questions. *How many...?* (Present Perfect Simple – quantity). *How long...?* (Present Perfect Continuous – duration).
  ● Students answer question.
  Use the Present Perfect Continuous to focus on an activity.

  Refer students to Pocket Book p. 8.

Practice **①** Tell students to refer to the grammar rules while doing this exercise if they need to.
  ● Write prompts on board: *Action – Past to now? Quantity?*
  ● Students work through exercise in pairs, finding evidence for their choice – either action or quantity.
  ● Check answers, whole class. Ask students to say which use of Present Perfect Simple or Continuous each sentence shows, and whether there is a difference with the tense they use in their language.
  1 has been working
  2 has made
  3 has been designing
  4 has travelled
  5 has made
  ● Ask students to underline the time expressions in the sentences. Stress that they all show a period up to the present.

since and *for*
- Students read examples and complete rule.
- Check answer, whole class.

⊙⚯ Use *since* with a point of time and *for* with a length of time.
- Look at timeline. Elicit further examples.

2 Students complete phrases individually.
- Check answers, whole class.

⊙⚯ 1 for   3 since   5 since   7 for   9 for
    2 for   4 since   6 since   8 since   10 since

Follow-up activity Spot test. Students test each other on exercise 2 in pairs.

3 Students complete article in pairs.
- Check answers, whole class.

⊙⚯ 1 have been   3 have become   5 started   7 has grown
    2 have been growing   4 have made   6 has increased

 Resource file 7.1, 7.2

4 Before students start exercise, practise question and answer with 'classroom' items: *How long have you had your (book/pen/bag, etc.)?* Draw attention to pronunciation of *have* /həv/ in question.

⚠️ Form. Remind students *Have you got...?* = Present tense. Present Perfect = *Have you had...?*

- After students have finished interviews, ask them to report back with two interesting/surprising pieces of information.

Pronunciation **①** Play tape twice. Check answer to question.
7.2 📼 ⊙⚯ Listener b. sounds more interested.
- Write *Have you?* and *Really?* twice each on board. ↘
- Play tape again. Mark intonation pattern for a. (fall–down)

↘↗

and b. (fall–rise down/up)

on board. Students repeat pattern b. only. Model in an exaggerated way, if necessary.
- Stress that reacting to what you hear during a conversation is very important.

7.3 📼 **②** Play tape once. Students tick conversations.
- Play tape again, if necessary. Check answers, whole class.

⊙⚯ 1, 3, 4, and 5.

7.4 📼 **③** Play tape, pausing after each conversation. Students repeat.
- Students practise conversations in pairs.
- Look at conversations in 2 again, and ask students when they use *Do you? Did you?* and *Have you?* Explain/elicit that these echo questions use the normal auxiliary verb for the tense.

Follow-up activity Students work in pairs. Student A tells partner about two things they do, two things they have done, and two things they did. Student B shows interest. Then change.

---

5 Read example questions together, then elicit possible questions from prompts.
- Students work in pairs (AA, BB) to prepare further questions.

6 Students do role-play in AB, AB pairs, then report back in their previous pairs.
- Students can repeat role-play, changing roles.

Wordpower 1 Draw a mini-graph on board and elicit vocabulary students already know.

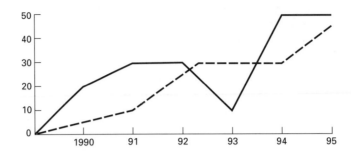

- Check vocabulary: *level off, reach a peak, remain stable*
- Students match verb phrases in pairs.
- Check answers, whole class.

 1 to go up, to increase   3 to level off   5 to reach a peak
2 to remain stable   4 to go down, to decrease, to fall   6 to improve

2 Tell students to use a dictionary for this exercise, if necessary.
- Check answers, whole class.

Verb   **Noun**

Infinitive	Past	
to decrease	decreased	a decrease
to fall	fell	a fall
to increase	increased	an increase
to rise	rose	a rise
to improve	improved	an improvement

- Draw students' attention to shifting stress in noun/verb pronunciation,

 to in*crease* but *an* **in**crease,   to de*crease* but *a* **de**crease.

- Practise pronunciation.

3 Students do exercise in pairs.
Dramatically. Emphasize that this can have positive as well as negative connotations.
- Check answers, whole class.

dramatic/dramatically   sudden, very large
sharp/sharply   sudden, large
steady/steadily   regular (not sudden)
slight/slightly   very small

- Check by drawing second graph on board. Ask students to label lines with descriptive adverbs.

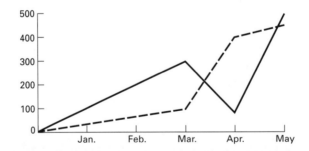

- Do further practice of adjective/adverb. Give the adjective in a sentence, *There was a sharp fall in prices,* to elicit *Prices fell sharply.* Then change and give the adverb to elicit the adjective.

4 Read examples. Draw attention to *rise/increase* + *in* + noun (*an increase in taxation*), + *of* + number (*an increase of 3%*).
- Students complete sentences individually.
- Check answers, whole class.

1 by   2 at   3 from, to   4 of   5 in

⑤ Students complete description in pairs.
- Check answers, whole class.

🔑 1 increased/rose/went up   3 reached a peak   5 fall/decrease
   2 increase/rise   4 sharply   6 fell/decreased/went down

⑥ Students prepare exercise in pairs, then write individually.
Follow-up activity Write on board *salaries, inflation, income tax, unemployment, the cost of living*. Ask students to describe changes/trends in their country in the past month/year/three years, etc.

Skills focus **①** Check vocabulary: *clothing, trade surplus* (value of exports greater than value of imports), *trade deficit* (value of imports greater than value of exports), *market, revenue, boom, textiles, footwear, labour costs*
- Encourage students to guess answers to questions.
- Students read text, then answer questions in pairs.
- Check answers, whole class.

🔑 1 Milan   2 400   3 surplus

② Check vocabulary in headings of EuroDatabank.
- Students complete tables.
- Ask students to find two pieces of information which surprise them.

🔑
A	Total value	$30b
B	Germany	94.5m
	France	48.2m
	USA	29.7m
C	Asia	60.4%
	W Europe	11.9%
	E Europe	11.2%
D	Germany	23.1%
	France	11.4%
	USA	9.8%
E	Italy	$6b
	Germany	$5.6b
	UK	$3.7b
	France	$3.3b

③ Divide class into groups.
- Groups appoint chairperson and spokesperson.
- Groups give feedback on their discussion.

④ Presentations can be given to whole class, or small groups. Agree a time limit for the presentation before students begin their preparation.

Social English **①** Check students remember James Turner writes for *Wine and Dine*.
- Give students time to read questions. Check vocabulary: *celebrate, anniversary, charter a plane*
7.5 🔊
- Play tape.
- Students note answers to questions.
- Check answers, whole class.

🔑 1 The tenth anniversary of *Wine and Dine* magazine.
   2 Because Scotland is too far for people to travel.
   3 The publication of James's book on Italian wines.
   4 He thinks it's a wonderful idea.

② Give students time to read through phrases.
- Practise pronunciation.
7.5 🔊
- Play tape again. Students tick phrases they hear.
- Students check answers in pairs.

🔑 **Asking for opinions**
What do you think about...?
What's your opinion of...?
How do you feel about...?

Giving opinions
In my opinion...
I think...
Agreeing
I agree.
I certainly agree with that.

7.6 ▣ ❸ Give students time to read through statements. Check vocabulary: *treasure hunt*
- Play tape. Students tick T or F.
- Check answers, whole class.

⊙⌐ 1 T   2 F   3 F   4 T

7.6 ▣ ❹ Give students time to read through phrases.
- Practise pronunciation.
- Play tape again. Students tick phrases they hear.
- Students check answers in pairs.

⊙⌐**Making suggestions**
I suggest...
How about...?
Why don't we...?
Why not...?
We could...
Asking for suggestions
Do you have any suggestions for...?
Accepting suggestions
Yes, let's do that.
Rejecting suggestions
I'm not sure about that.

❺ Write on board: *go to London? go to London. going to London?*
Draw students' attention to *-ing* form of verb after *How about...?* and *What about...?*, and infinitive without *to* after *Why not...?* Also word order in *Why don't we...?*
- Practise pronunciation.
- Students do matching exercise in pairs.
- Check answers, whole class.

⊙⌐ (Possible answers)
I suggest we go skiing next weekend.
How about buying tickets for the music festival?
What about going away for a few days?
Why don't we invite some friends for dinner?
Why not spend next Sunday in the country?
We could go to a restaurant in the evening.
- Oral practice. Give prompts of second half of sentence: *meeting this evening? have lunch early. go to Rome. eating out?* Students complete sentences.
- Ask students to make their own suggestions. Prompt if necessary: *Any ideas on... (what to do after class)?*

❻ Divide class into groups.
- Monitor group work.

❼ Divide class into new groups.
- Monitor group work.
- Groups report back on their suggestions.

  Resource file 7.3, 7.4

Tapescript Unit 7

7.1

P=Radio presenter, S=Susan Hill

P Hello, and welcome to another programme in our series, *Working abroad*. Our guest this evening is an English person who lives and works in Italy. Her name is Susan Hill... Susan, welcome to the programme. You live in one of Italy's most famous cities – Florence. How long have you been living there?

S I've been living in Florence since 1982. But when I went there in 1982, I planned to stay for only six months.

P Why did you change your mind?

S Well, I'm a designer. I design leather goods, mainly shoes and handbags. Soon after I arrived in Florence, I got a job with one of Italy's top fashion houses, Ferragamo – so I decided to stay!

P How lucky! Do you still work for Ferragamo?

S No. I've been a freelance designer for quite a long time now, since 1988, in fact.

P So does that mean you design for several different companies now?

S Yes, that's right. Since I went freelance, I've designed a lot of fashion items for Italian companies. And in the last four years, I've also been designing for the British company, Burberrys.

P What have you been designing for them?

S Mostly handbags and small leather goods.

P Has the fashion industry in Italy changed since 1982?

S Oh, yes. It's become a lot more competitive – because the quality of products from other countries has improved a lot. But Italian quality and design is still world-famous.

P And do you ever think of returning to live in England?

S No, not really. I've made a lot of important contacts in the fashion industry, and for a freelance designer, working in Italy is a lot easier, and more interesting! And, of course, it's not only the work – I really love the sun and the lifestyle!

P Have you been to England this year?

S No. I haven't had time. I've been travelling a lot recently. I've just visited a factory in Modena, for example, and I've been to Germany a few times since Christmas.

P And have you had any free time in your busy work schedule?

S Well, unfortunately, I've had very little free time this year, but I've been visiting friends more in the last few months. I feel that I've been working too much this year, so I've been trying to relax more...

P Well, thank you for talking to us, Susan.

S It was a pleasure.

7.2

a. I've lived here for fifteen years. Have you? (↘)

b. I've lived here for fifteen years. Have you? (↘↗)

a. I work in Helsinki. Really? (↘)

b. I work in Helsinki. Really? (↘↗)

7.3

1 I work in the city centre.
  Do you?
2 I didn't have time to finish the book yesterday.
  Didn't you?
3 I've been working very hard this week.
  Have you?
4 I don't like jazz.
  Don't you?
5 We went to a restaurant for lunch.
  Did you?
6 I've never visited Rome.
  Haven't you?

7.4

1 I often travel on business.
  Do you?
2 I didn't speak to him last week.
  Didn't you?
3 I've been living here for ages.
  Have you?
4 I don't eat meat.
  Don't you?
5 We visited all the major cities last year.
  Did you?
6 I've never been to the opera.
  Haven't you?

7.5

J=James, D=Duncan

J Sorry I'm late, Duncan. The traffic was terrible...

D Oh, don't apologize. I'm glad you could find time for a meeting.

J OK, so you want to discuss how we celebrate the tenth anniversary of *Wine and Dine*, right?

D Yes. First, what do you think about having the celebration at my castle in Scotland, instead of at a London hotel?

J Well, in my opinion, Scotland is too far for people to travel.

D Yes, I agree. So I thought of chartering a plane from London. We could include travel to Scotland in the invitation. What's your opinion of that?

J I think that's a really great idea!

D Good. Second, how do you feel about celebrating the publication of your new book on Italian wines at the same time?

J That's a wonderful idea, Duncan! I certainly agree with that.

D I thought you'd like that idea! Now, we need to decide on the programme. What do you think about this idea...

7.6

D=Duncan, J=James

D OK, James. Then I suggest you give a talk on Italian wines.

J How about having a tasting of Italian wines?

D Yes, let's do that. Right, that's a very full programme on the first day. Do you have any suggestions for the second day?

J Why don't we make the second day more relaxing? Give people an opportunity to socialize, to get to know each other better. Why not start the day with a champagne breakfast?

D Yes, and we could follow that with a treasure hunt in the garden, with a bottle of something very special as the treasure?

J Hmm, I'm not sure about that. What if it rains?

D Don't worry, James. We have wonderful summers in Scotland. And then people can choose – there's tennis, swimming, golf.

J In fact everything for a great weekend of celebration!

D That's right. And we finish with a big party in the evening. Well, James, I think we've agreed on everything. All we need now is to check the guest list, and make sure we haven't forgotten anyone...

UNIT 8

Language focus   p. 66

Futures: Present Continuous and *going to*

1, 2   Discussion and reading: luxury hotel features.
3–5   Preparation and listening: plans and arrangements
       for a hotel opening.   8.1, 8.2 ⬛
       Grammar analysis: Present Continuous,   p. 9 📘
          going to.

Practice   p. 68

1, 2   Gap-fill: fax. Describe arrangements.
3, 4   Making appointments.   p. 20 📘
5   New Year resolutions.   8.1
       Pronunciation: stressed and unstressed *to*. 8.3, 8.4 ⬛
6   Pairwork interview: travel plans.
7   Groupwork: plan a visit and present plans.   8.2
                                                     p. 48 📘

Wordpower   p. 72

Air travel

1   Complete a word map.
2   Game: guess the word.   8.3, 8.4
                                                p. 52

Skills focus   p. 73

Listening. Travelling by air

1   Airlines.   p. 28 📘
2–4   Announcements at an airport.   8.5, 8.6 ⬛
5–7   Announcements on a plane.   8.7 ⬛
8   Discussion: flying.
9   Project: short talk or article on air travel or airlines.

Social English   p. 75

Invitations

1–3   Inviting someone to stay.   8.8, 8.9 ⬛
4   Role-play: invitations.   p. 21 📘   8.5
                                                p. 53

Language focus **1** Elicit suggestions for facilities. List on board.

⚷ (Possible answers)

restaurants, bars, sports facilities, laundry services, business centre with computers, fax, e-mail, photocopier, etc.

2 Students read brochure. Ask them to add any further facilities to the list.
- Discuss answer to question, whole class.

3 Check vocabulary: *press briefing, reception, balloon flights, musical extravaganza*
- Students read invitation and programme, then prepare questions in pairs. Note at this stage if students make questions using a future form, as a diagnostic check.
- Write some of the questions students suggest on board.

8.1 **4** Students read Nick Lander's questions.
- Play tape. Students check if journalists asked any of the questions they suggested in 3.
- Students note what they remember from first listening.
- Play tape again, if necessary.
- Check answers, whole class.

⚷ 1 No, he's arriving by helicopter.
2 In the Conference Room on the first floor.
3 In the garden.
4 No, he isn't.

8.2 **5** Give students time to read incomplete statements. Ask them to predict answers.
- Play tape. Students note answers.
- Play tape again, if necessary.
- Check answers, whole class.

⚷ 1 flight
2 the President's arrival
3 business facilities
4 business people
5 Roof Garden, Oriental cuisine

Futures: Present Continuous, *going to*
- Students read examples and complete rules in pairs.
- Check answers, whole class.

⚷ Use the Present Continuous for fixed future arrangements.
Use *going to* for future plans, intentions, and decisions.

Refer students to Pocket Book p. 9.

Practice **1** Students complete Nick's fax individually.
- Check answers, whole class.

⚷ 1 I'm arriving
2 I'm travelling
3 I'm having
4 I'm interviewing
5 I'm spending

2 Students ask and answer questions about Nick's arrangements in pairs. Practise question forms before they begin, if necessary. Remind students of different intonation patterns in *Wh-* and closed questions.

⚷ (Possible answers)

21 July – he's going on a sightseeing tour of the city.
22 July – he's having dinner with Kiki Johns.
23 July – he's meeting exporters at the Trade Centre.

3 Review phrases for making arrangements. Refer students to Pocket Book p. 20.
- Students complete their diary.

4 Divide class into groups.
- Model example dialogue with one student. Make sure they know they must give reasons for being unable to meet.

5 Explain 'New Year resolution', if necessary, then set time limit while individuals prepare ideas.
- Students explain their resolutions, whole class.

 Resource file 8.1

Pronunciation ① Remind students of sound 'schwa' in unstressed syllables (Unit 5). (*computer, arrangement,* etc.)

8.3   • Play tape once or twice. Check answer to question.

   ⊙⟞ The strong form is in sentence a.

8.4 ② Play tape. Students mark which sound they hear, a. or b.

    • Play tape again, pausing after each sentence to check answers.

   ⊙⟞ 1 b.   2 b.   3 a.   4 b.   5 b.   6 a.

8.4 ③ Play tape again. Students repeat sentences.

    • Students work in pairs to complete rule.

    • Check answer, whole class.

   ⊙⟞ Use the strong form of *to* when the word is at the end of a sentence.

④ Students work in pairs to match question and answers, then practise pronunciation in pairs.

⑥ Students prepare questions in pairs, AA, BB.

    • Pairs interview each other, AB, AB.

    • Students report back on two things about their partner's travel plans, whole class.

❼ Briefly review phrases for making suggestions. Refer students to Pocket Book p. 20.

    • Students read 'Congratulations' note. Make sure they understand the time constraints for their stay.

    • Divide class into groups.

    • Monitor group work.

    • Students present their group plan.

RF   Resource file 8.2

Wordpower   • With students' books closed, write heading *Air travel* on board. Students work in pairs to list as many words connected with the topic as possible. Set time limit of five minutes.

    • Write suggested words on board. Encourage students to group them into categories, and to give each category a sub-heading.

❶ Students complete word map individually.

    • Check answers, whole class.

   ⊙⟞ Terminal: passport control, duty-free shop, security check, arrivals board, customs, information desk. Luggage: briefcase, suitcase, trolley. Documents: ticket, boarding card. On board: overhead locker, seat-belt, life-jacket, window seat, flight attendant.

❷ Divide class into groups.

    • Use example to demonstrate activity. Make sure students realize they can only answer *yes* or *no*.

RF   Resource file 8.3, 8.4

Skills focus ❶ If you expect students may have difficulty with this task, elicit and write some airline names on the board: *British Airways, Lufthansa, Alitalia, Qantas, Air Canada, Air France, Sabena.* Explain that initial letters are usually used in flight identifiers. They should then be able to do task.

    • Students complete tables in groups. Refer them to Pocket Book p. 28.

    • Check answers, whole class. Practise spelling by asking students to spell nationalities.

   ⊙⟞

AF 645	Air France	French	LH 4980	Lufthansa	German
AZ 1420	Alitalia	Italian	IB 3765	Iberia	Spanish
MA 732	Malev	Hungarian	OA 287	Olympic	Greek

    • Review names of countries.

❷ Identify settings, whole class. Practise pronunciation.

   ⊙⟞ 1 P   2 C   3 P   4 C/A   5 C/A   6 A   7 C   8 A

8.5 🔳 **3** Look at the air travel information. Check vocabulary: *destination*, *last call*
 - Play tape. Students complete information.
 - Students check answers in pairs.
 - Play tape again, if necessary.
 - Check answers, whole class.

AF 962	11.15	Marseilles	Boarding	11
LH 4037	11.25	Dusseldorf	Boarding	28
IB 3915	11.50	Malaga	Delayed	10
AZ 287	11.45	Venice	Last call	15
OA 259	11.45	Athens	Last call	19

8.6 🔳 **4** Students read descriptions. Check vocabulary: *security*
 - Play tape, pausing after each announcement for students to write number.
 - Play tape again, pausing to check answers.

1 b.   2 a.   3 d.   4 c.   5 e.

5 Students match sentences in pairs.

1 d.   2 b.   3 f.   4 a.   5 c.   6 e.

8.7 🔳 **6** Play tape. Students check answers.

7 Students find synonyms individually.
 - Check answers, whole class.

| 1 shortly | 3 remain seated | 5 to fill in |
| 2 are required to | 4 in the upright position | 6 has come to a complete standstill |

8 Divide class into groups.
 - Give groups time to brainstorm possible questions.
 - Form new groups to do the activity.

9 Students prepare the talk or the article as a group activity in class.

Social English **1** Check vocabulary: *invite*, *invitation*, *accept*, *decline*
 - Elicit phrases students know for inviting, accepting, and declining. Prompt with questions: *You want to invite someone to dinner, what do you say? You can't accept an invitation, what do you say?* etc.
 - Students read invitation. Check: *RSVP (Répondez s'il vous plaît = reply, please)*

8.8 🔳
 - Play tape.
 - Check answers, whole class.

1 He invites Monique to stay at Glencross after the celebration.
2 She agrees to stay.
 - Play tape again, if necessary.

8.9 🔳 **2** Play tape.
 - Check answers, whole class.

1 Because he's going to be very busy.
2 Duncan tells him that Monique is going to stay.

8.8, 8.9 🔳 **3** Give students time to read through phrases.
 - Practise pronunciation.
 - Play both tape dialogues again. Students tick phrases.
 - Check answers, whole class.

Inviting	**Accepting**
I'd like to invite you to...	Thank you. I'd be delighted to accept.
Would you join us...?	Thank you. I'd love to.
Would you like to...?	**Declining**
How about...?	I'd love to, but (*I'm afraid I can't*).

 - Point out that we usually give a reason when we decline an invitation, in order not to seem impolite.

4 Monitor pairwork.
 Follow-up activity Ask students to write down the ideas they had for extra situations for role-play. Swap with other pairs for further practice.

 Resource file 8.5

Tapescript Unit 8

8.1 🔘

P=Press Officer, N=Nick Lander, K=Kiki Johns

P Good evening. My name is Julie Waite. Welcome to the Pacific Hotel and to this press briefing. I know you want more information about tomorrow's Grand Opening, so let's begin with your questions.

N Could you give us more details about the President's arrival?

P Yes. The President is arriving by helicopter at 10 a.m.

N Right. And where is he making the opening speech?

P In the Conference Room on the first floor. But we're not having the champagne reception there, that's taking place in the garden, from eleven to eleven thirty.

K What exactly is the Oriental menu presentation at 14.00?

P Two of our chefs are presenting our special 'Oriental menu' – that's the menu we serve in the Oriental Restaurant.

N Is the President taking a balloon flight in the afternoon?

P No, he isn't. The balloon flights are for journalists and TV cameramen. If you'd like to take one of the flights, please give me your name after this briefing.

N/K/other journalists Oh, yes. What a great idea!

P Any more questions about tomorrow's programme? No? Then let's go on to the next part of our briefing…

8.2 🔘

N=Nick Lander, K=Kiki Johns

N What a wonderful idea! Are you going to take a balloon flight?

K Yes, of course. Think of the fantastic photos we can get from the air, the Roof Garden, the swimming pool.

N Yes. And I'm going to take photos of the President's arrival by helicopter, on the hotel roof.

K Good idea. What are you going to write about?

N Oh, everything. It's such a marvellous hotel. I'm going to write a lot about the business facilities. They're the best I've ever seen – the latest technology, the fastest communication links. That's very important for the readers of my magazine – they're all business people, you see. What about you?

K Well, I'm definitely not going to describe the hotel's business facilities! My readers come to a hotel like this for a holiday, not for work! No, I'm going to write about the leisure facilities, the Roof Garden, and the oriental cuisine…

8.3 🔘

a. Who do I speak to?   b. Can I speak to John?

8.4 🔘

Example You can speak to him tomorrow.   b.
1 We're going to see him tomorrow.
2 Did you listen to the news this morning?
3 Paolo is a man you can talk to.
4 You can write to me at my office.
5 You can talk to Paolo.
6 What address do I write to?

8.5 🔘

Air France flight 962 to Marseilles is now ready for boarding. Please proceed to Gate number 11. Gate 11 for flight AF 962 to Marseilles.

Passengers travelling to Dusseldorf on Lufthansa flight 4037 are requested to proceed to Gate number 28. Flight LH 4037, now boarding at Gate number 28.

Iberia Airways regret to announce the delay of flight IB 3915 to Malaga. This flight is now scheduled to leave at 11.50.

Final call for Alitalia flight 287 to Venice. Please go immediately to Gate 15.

This is the final call for Olympic Airways flight 259 to Athens. This flight is now closing at Gate 19.

8.6 🔘

1 Your attention, please. Would Mrs van Slooten, travelling to Amsterdam, please contact the KLM information desk.

2 We are now ready to board. Would passengers in seat rows 17 to 22 board first. Please have your boarding cards ready.

3 Your attention, please. Will the person who left a black briefcase in the transfer security area please return there to collect it immediately.

4 May I have your attention, please. This is a special announcement. Will Mr Balmain, the last remaining passenger for flight SR 836 to Geneva, please go immediately to Gate 5, where his aircraft is waiting to depart.

5 May I have your attention, please. This is a security announcement. Passengers are reminded not to leave their bags unattended at any time.

8.7 🔘

1 Please fasten your seat-belts.
2 Smoking is not allowed in rows 1 to 6 and 10 to 22, and in the toilets.
3 Please make sure your seat is in the upright position for take-off.
4 We will shortly be serving drinks and a light meal.
5 Non-EU passengers are required to fill in a landing card.
6 Please remain seated until the aircraft has come to a complete standstill.

8.8 🔘

D=Duncan Ross, M=Monique Bresson

D Hello. Duncan Ross.

M Hello, Duncan. It's Monique Bresson. My secretary said you called.

D Yes. Thank you for calling back. I wanted to make sure you've received the invitation.

M Yes, I have. Thank you. I'd be delighted to accept.

D Good. Er… Monique, some friends of mine are going to stay at Glencross for a few days after the celebration, and I'd like to invite you to stay, too. Would you join us for four or five days?

M Oh, I'd love to, Duncan, but I'm afraid I can't. I've already arranged to go to Brussels on the 18th…

D Well, would you like to stay until the 17th? I'm sure you need a break from your busy schedule. You work too much, Monique!

M You're right. Thank you, Duncan, I'd love to stay until the 17th.

8.9 🔘

J=James Turner, D=Duncan Ross

J Hello.

D Hello, James, it's Duncan. How's everything? I hope you're ready for the big event at Glencross!

J Not yet, but there's still time.

D James, some friends are going to stay at Glencross for a few days after the celebration. How about joining us?

J Thanks a lot, Duncan, I'd love to, but I'm going to be very busy during that week.

D That's a pity. Monique Bresson is going to stay and I know you enjoy her company.

J Is she really? Then let me think about it, Duncan, perhaps I can manage to change a few appointments…

UNIT 9

Language focus   p. 80

Future: *will*, 1st Conditional, *if* and *when*

1   Discussion and reading: high-speed trains.
2   Reading: future train travel.
3   Identify verbs in text referring to future.

     Grammar analysis: Future: *will*,
     1st Conditional, *if* and *when*.   p. 10,11 PB

Practice   p. 82

1   Write questions based on the text.
     Pronunciation: /ɪ/ contrasted with /iː/   9.1, 9.2
2   Pairwork: question and answer.
3   Pairwork: interviews about future activities.   9.1 RF
4   Make predictions.
5   Sentence completion.
6   Speculation.
7   Describing plans.   9.2 RF
8   Discussion: travel in the future.   p. 54 WB

Wordpower   p. 85

Train travel

1   Identifying station signs.
2   Collocation: complete chart.
3   Complete collocation matrix.
4   Group work: prepare and carry out a rail   9.3 RF
     transport survey.   p. 58 WB

Skills focus   p. 86

Listening. Personal computing

1   Reading: preparation.
2   Product briefing: a new small computer.   9.3
3–5 Group work: research survey.
6   Project: 'design' a computer.   9.4 RF

Social English   p. 88

Offers and requests

1–3 Asking someone to arrange a trip.   9.4, 9.5
4   Role-play: offers.
5   Role-play: requests.
6   Role-play: offers and requests.   p. 21 PB   p. 59 WB

Language focus ❶ Discuss answer to question, whole class. Encourage students to ask each other follow-up questions: *When? Where from? How fast?* etc.
- Set a time limit for students to read extracts and note interesting facts.
- Answer any vocabulary questions.
- Whole group feedback on interesting points from each extract.

❷ Check vocabulary: *a proposal, (pan-European) train network, a suburb, (traffic) congestion, to achieve a speed*
- Students read text and answer questions.
- Check answers, whole class.

   1 It's a proposal for a high-speed European train network.
   2 In 1981.
   3 On many routes, the airlines have lost up to 90% of their passengers to the trains.
- Ask students their opinion of the CER proposal.

❸ Students read through text and underline verbs individually.
- Ask students to read out some of the verbs they have underlined.
Use this as an opportunity to see how aware they are of the form.

   (Possible answers)
   will revolutionize   will take   will be   'll choose   'll find

Future: *will*, 1st Conditional, *if* and *when*
- Students read examples for Future: *will*.
- Students complete grammar rule in pairs.
- Check answers, whole class.

   Use *will* + infinitive to predict future situations and actions.
We can use both *going to* and *will* in future predictions. *How many people are going to attend the conference?* and *How many people will attend?* are interchangeable. For the major differences between *will* and *going to*, see Pocket Book p. 9 and 10.

Refer students to Pocket Book p. 10.

- Students read examples for 1st Conditional, *if* and *when*.
- Students complete rules, in pairs.
- Check answers, whole class.

   To make the 1st Conditional, use *if* + the Present Simple, + *will* + infinitive.
Use the 1st Conditional to express a future possibility and its result.
Use *if* to express a possibility, and *when* to express a certainty.

Refer students to Pocket Book p. 11.

Practice ❶ Use example to demonstrate that students need to refer back to text to find noun phrases.
- Students complete questions in pairs.
- Check answers, whole class.

   (Possible answers)
   1 How long will train journeys between major cities take?
   2 How long will the journey from Brussels to Paris take?
   3 How many types of line will there be?
   4 Which method of travel will business people choose?
   5 What will the 21st century be?

Pronunciation This minimal pair may not represent a problem for all nationalities, but practice will raise awareness that individual sounds can affect meaning.

9.1 ① Play tape. Students repeat words to identify sounds.
- If necessary, practise individual sounds /ɪ/ and /iː/.

9.2 ② Play tape. Students write which sound they hear, a. or b.
- Play tape again, pausing after each word to check answers.
⊙━ 1 a. 2 b. 3 a. 4 b. 5 b. 6 b. 7 a. 8 a.

9.2 ③ Play tape again, pausing after each word for students to repeat.

❷ Read example questions and refer to the information on the map.
- Practise pronunciation: *it'll, they'll*
- Students ask and answer questions in pairs.
- Monitor pairwork.

❸ Check students understand model answers: *Yes, definitely,* etc.
- Practise pronunciation: *Do you think you'll...?*
I don't think so but *I hope not.*
- After pairwork interviews, ask students to report back on three of their partner's future actions.

Resource file 9.1

❹ Make predictions with whole class. Encourage follow-up and reaction questions: *Do you think so? What makes you think that? Are you sure?*

❺ Remind students of the use of the Present Simple in the *if* clause in the 1st Conditional.
- Check vocabulary: *to close down, to lose an election, to expand, to make a loss*
- Students write completion of sentences individually.
- Ask some students to read out their sentences.

❻ Work through exercise with whole class. Elicit as many different solutions as possible for each problem.

❼ Before doing the exercise, ask: *What are your plans for this evening? tomorrow? the weekend?* Remind students to use *going to* or Present Continuous for their plans and arrangements.
- Demonstrate the exercise with one student. Encourage students to think of as many *What will you do if...?* questions as possible.

Resource file 9.2

❽ Divide class into groups.
- Monitor group discussion.
- Groups report back on their discussion.

Wordpower ❶ Students answer questions in pairs.
- Check answers, whole class.
⊙━ 1 Information
2 Left luggage
3 Tickets
4 Lost property
5 Waiting room
6 Platforms 1–3
7 Departures
8 Buffet
9 Customer services
- Practise, if necessary, by asking simple questions: *Why are you going to the (Buffet)?*

2 Students complete charts individually.
- Students check answers in pairs.
- Check answers, whole class.

 train/plane/taxi fare
day return/period return ticket
monthly/annual season ticket
underground/intercity trains

3 Students complete grid individually.
- Check answers, whole class.

 to catch/miss a plane/a bus
to drive a train/a bus/a coach/a car/a taxi
to ride a bicycle/a motorbike
to get on/off a plane/a train/a bus/a bicycle/a motorbike
to get into/out of a car/a taxi
to take a plane/a train/a bus/a coach/a taxi

Follow-up activity Students describe recent journeys on different modes of transport. Ask prompt questions: *What time did you catch the train? Did you take a bus to the station?* etc.

get on/off forms of public transport, but *into/out of* cars and taxis.

take a car = take a car from the pool available (therefore unusual), *take **the** car* = take my/our car.

4 Divide class into groups to prepare survey.
- Monitor pairwork.
- Students report back on their interviews.

Follow-up activity Students work in pairs or small groups to create a word map on *Transport.* They then compare their word maps with the rest of the class.

 Resource file 9.3

Skills focus **1** With students' books closed, write the title *The electronic personal assistant* on the board. Ask students to speculate what the text will include.
- Check vocabulary: *to recognize, handwriting, graphics, to schedule, to remind*
- Students read text and answer question.
- Find out if students know of other products which are like the Newton MessagePad. If so, ask them to describe them briefly.

9.3 **2** Read questions; ask students to speculate about possible answers.
- Write some of students' suggestions on board.
- Check vocabulary: *keyboard, screen, printer, electronic mail, (e-mail)*
- Play tape once.
- Students compare answers in pairs.
- Play tape again, if necessary.
- Check answers, whole class.

 (Possible answers)
1 Because you simply write on it with a pen.
2 By phone, fax, or by electronic mail.
3 Yes.

3 Divide class into groups. Set a time limit for preparation of survey.

4 Monitor pairwork.

5 Set a time limit for preparation and presentation. Groups present their opinions and reasons.

6 Students could also design and write a promotional leaflet for their computer.

 Resource file 9.4

❶ Elicit phrases students know for offers and requests. Prompt with questions: *What do you say if you see someone carrying a lot of books? If you need help with an exercise?*

9.4
- Play tape once. Students note down information.
- Students compare information in pairs.
- Play tape again, if necessary.
- Check answers, whole class.

⚷ Book flight   Edinburgh – Paris on Sunday afternoon/evening
Book hotel   Paris – three nights
Get information about   plane and train to Bordeaux on Wednesday

9.5 ❷ Play tape.
- Students answer questions in pairs.
- Check answers, whole class.

⚷ 1 By direct flight from Bordeaux.
2 Because he's going to stay with some friends.

9.4, 9.5 ❸ Give students time to read phrases.
- Practise pronunciation.
- Play two conversations again.
- Students tick phrases.
- Students check answers in pairs.

⚠ Response to *Do you mind...? No = OK, go ahead.*

⚷ **Requesting**   **Agreeing**
Can you...?   Yes, of course.
Could you...?   Yes, certainly.
Would you mind... (+ *-ing*)?   No, of course not.
Do you think you could...?

Offering   **Accepting**
Shall I...?   Yes, please.
Do you want me to...?   Thank you. I'd appreciate that.
Would you like me to...?   **Declining**
      Thanks, but that won't be necessary.

❹ Students practise in pairs.
- Follow up with quick whole class practice of the same situations. Nominate students at random to make an offer and respond.

❺ Follow same procedure as for 4.

❻ Students work with a different partner for this pairwork.
- Ask students to keep a note of the additional situations they think of. Practise them with whole class.

Tapescript Unit 9

9.1
1 a. printer   b. Sweden

9.2
Example   will   *a.*
1 still   5 please
2 three   6 key
3 trip   7 visit
4 speed   8 grilled

9.3
C=Clive Girling, Product Marketing Manager for Apple Computer UK

C The first thing I'd like to say about the Newton MessagePad is that it's as easy to use as pencil and paper. It doesn't have a keyboard like a computer, you simply write on the screen with a pen. The Newton reads your handwriting and changes it into typed text. And it recognizes pictures as well, so you can draw maps and diagrams, for example.
Second, the Newton MessagePad is very personal. It learns about you – your daily programme, your meetings, your friends. It helps you to organize your life, like a personal assistant. For example, if you write on the MessagePad 'lunch with John, Tuesday', it'll find the information about 'John' in the Name file. Then it'll write the lunch appointment in the Date Book for the next Tuesday, at the time you usually have lunch.
Third, the Newton helps you to communicate. For example, if you want to phone John about the lunch appointment, it'll dial his phone number for you. If you prefer to send John a fax, with a map of the restaurant, then you can do that too, using a standard telephone line, or you can connect your Newton to a printer and send John a printed letter. Your Newton can also communicate with other computers by electronic mail.
So, I hope that gives you some idea of the ways you can communicate with other people using the Newton. But there are hundreds of other things you can do with your Newton, using the different software applications on the market. And of course, a company can produce its own software and use the Newton to do particular jobs in that company. I think the Newton MessagePad really is the beginning of a new age in telecommunications and personal computing.

9.4
D=Duncan Ross, C=Carol, Duncan's secretary

D (*phone*) Oh, Carol, can you come into my office? It's about my trip to France.
C Yes, of course. (*Carol arrives*) So, you have meetings in Paris on Monday and Tuesday.
D Yes. I'll be in Scotland at Glencross the week before, so could you book me a flight from Edinburgh to Paris on Sunday afternoon or evening if possible?
C Right. Shall I book a hotel in Paris for those three nights?
D Yes, please. Then on Wednesday I want to travel to Bordeaux, either by train or plane.
C Would you like me to get some information on both?
D Thank you. I'd appreciate that. I need to be in Bordeaux by about 1 p.m. I think the TGV is probably best. Would you mind checking arrival times of the TGV and the plane?
C No, of course not.
D Right, thanks very much, Carol. That's all for the moment. I'm not sure about the trip back yet, but we can arrange that later.

9.5
D (*phone*) Carol, I'd like to give you the other details about my trip to France.
C Yes, fine. I'll come in.
D Right, I need to be back in London on the Friday evening. Do you think you could check the times of direct flights from Bordeaux?
C Yes, certainly. What about accommodation? Do you want me to book you a hotel in Bordeaux?
D Thanks, but that won't be necessary. I'm going to stay with some friends. They've got a little château and some vineyards, and they produce some very good wine.
C Mm, it sounds a lot more enjoyable than a hotel.
D Yes, I think it will be.

UNIT 10

Language focus   p. 90

2nd Conditional

1, 2   Discussion and reading: traffic problems.
3, 4   Listening: traffic problems and solutions.   **10.1** 🔘

      Grammar analysis: 2nd Conditional.
      Contrast 1st and 2nd Conditional.   p. 11, 12 📖

Practice   p. 91

1   Sentence completion.
2–4   Discussion: hypothetical situations.
5   Pairwork survey: a perfect weekend.   **10.1** RF
      Pronunciation: stress and rhythm in   p. 60 WB
      2nd Conditional sentences.   **10.2, 10.3** 🔘

Wordpower   p. 93

Prepositions of place, office equipment

1   Identify pictures: office equipment.
2   Describe location of objects.
3   Pairwork: describe and draw.   p. 64 WB

Skills focus   p. 94

Writing. Business correspondence

1   Letter-writing quiz.   p. 24, 25, 26 📖
2   Formal letters: identify functions of
      formulae.
3   Matching exercise: phrases and functions.
4   Gap-fill: formal letter.
5   Writing: reply to a letter.
6   Project: write a letter of enquiry.   **10.2, 10.3, 10.4** RF

Social English   p. 96

Telephoning: asking for information

1–4   Telephoning: asking for travel
      information.   **10.4, 10.5** 🔘
5–6   Practice: indirect questions.
7   Role-play: obtaining travel information.   p. 22 📖   p. 65 WB

● With students' books closed, write *Cities in Crisis*, *problems* and *solutions* on board. Elicit vocabulary relating to the problem of too many cars in cities. Include vocabulary from the extracts: *traffic jam, traffic congestion, traffic chaos, to ban cars, to take measures (to solve problems), emergency measures, pollution, breathing problems*. Check pronunciation.

1 Discuss questions, whole class. Add vocabulary to list on board as appropriate.

2 Students read extracts and work in pairs to list problems.
● Check lists, whole class.
● Discuss points, whole class.

⌕⟶ (Possible answers)

not enough parking spaces	double parking/streets blocked by parked cars
traffic jams	pollution
inadequate metro system	health problems
too many cars	

10.1 **3** Give students time to read through suggestions a. to d.
● Play tape. Students write number of caller.
● Check answers, whole class.

⌕⟶ a. Caller 3   b. Caller 2   c. Caller 1   d. Caller 4

10.1 **4** Students read T/F statements.
● Play tape again. Students tick T or F.
● Students check answers in pairs.
● Play tape a third time if necessary, pausing to check answers. Or check answers, whole class.

⌕⟶ 1 T   2 T   3 F   4 T

2nd Conditional
● Give students time to read examples.
● Students complete grammar rules in pairs.

⌕⟶ To make the 2nd Conditional, use *if* + Past Simple, + *would* or *could* + infinitive.

● Focus on use of past tense in *if* clause.
● Check concept with questions: *Are you the Transport Minister? Do motorists have to pay to use their cars? No, but if...*
● Check understanding of *could* (possibility or ability). *What would it be possible to do if we charged motorists* = could, would be able to. Could = both the past tense and the conditional of *can*.
● Students discuss answers to questions in pairs.

Refer students to Pocket Book p. 12.

Practice **1** Students complete sentences individually.
● Discuss answers, whole class.

2 Give students time to write down three points.
● Discuss points, whole class.

3 Students work together, then report to class on similarities or differences with their partner.

4 Give students enough time to think about their answers.
● Deal with one topic at a time, whole class.
● Encourage students to ask each other follow-up questions about their answers.

5 Students work in AA, BB pairs to prepare questions, then in AB pairs to carry out interview.
● Whole class feedback. Ask students to talk about two or three responses.

 Resource file 10.1

Pronunciation

This pronunciation practice is designed to raise awareness of the importance of stress and rhythm. It is an especially important area for those whose first language is syllable-timed, rather than stress-timed.

10.2 ① Play tape twice. Students mark main stress.
- Ask students what they notice about the stressed words. Explain/elicit main stress is placed on words carrying main meaning.

a. I'd do more <u>sport</u> if I had enough <u>time</u>.
b. If I earned more <u>money</u>, I'd buy a new <u>car</u>.

② Students work in pairs to mark stress on sentences.
1 If I had a <u>car</u>, I'd drive it to <u>work</u>.
2 If I lived in the <u>city</u>, I'd travel by <u>bike</u>.
3 I'd take more <u>exercise</u> if I were <u>you</u>.
4 If they banned all <u>cars</u>, the air would be <u>cleaner</u>.
5 If the buses were <u>quicker</u>, more people would <u>use</u> them.
6 Would you take the <u>train</u> if you <u>could</u>?

10.3 ③ Play tape. Students check answers.
- Play tape again. Students repeat.

④ Before students begin pairwork, practise pronunciation of question starters given.

Wordpower ❶ Set time limit (3 minutes) for students to match vocabulary to photos.
- Check answers, whole class.

9 ashtray   12 diary   14 phone   10 bookcase   18 filing cabinet
3 table lamp   2 chair   1 table   4 desk   11 clock
17 keyboard   5 photocopier   13 bin   6 coffee machine   15 year planner
7 computer   16 mouse   8 mineral water
- Practise pronunciation and spelling.

❷ Give students time to look at prepositions diagram.
- Practise with whole class. Name an object. Students describe its location.
- Individual students make false statements, others correct them, e.g. *The bookcase is next to the Year Planner. No, it isn't. It's under it.* etc.

❸ Students may want to make a simple sketch before they describe their room. Suggest they do not include too many items.
- If necessary, model an example yourself.

Skills focus ❶ Find out if students write letters in English. If so, to whom, what about, etc.
- Students answer quiz in pairs.
- Students check answers in Pocket Book pp. 24, 25, 26.

1 T   2 F   3 T   4 F   5 F   6 T   7 T   8 T

❷ Students find phrases individually, then check answers in pairs.
1 We have pleasure in enclosing…
2 Please contact us again if you would like any further information.
3 With reference to…
4 Unfortunately,…

❸ Explain term 'function'. *The function of 'hello' is to…* (greet).
- Students match functions and phrases in pairs.
- Check answers, whole class.

1 c.   2 e.   3 a.   4 d.   5 i.   6 b.   7 h.   8 g.   9 j.   10 f.

❹ Students complete letter individually.
- Check answers, whole class.

❺ Students draft letter in pairs, then write it individually in class, or as homework.
- Collect finished work and give feedback.

❻ Note: The British Council gives information on courses.

 Resource file 10.2, 10.3, 10.4

Social English **❶** Remind students of information Duncan Ross asked his secretary, Carol, to get in
Unit 9. (Flight times Edinburgh–Paris, train and flight times Paris–Bordeaux.)

10.4 🔲 • Play tape. Students note down information, then check information in pairs.
• Play tape again if necessary.

	Edinburgh	Paris		Bordeaux	London
Sun p.m.	14.45	18.45	Fri p.m.	14.40	15.10
	16.00	20.50			
	18.00	23.05			

10.4 🔲 **❷** Students read through phrases.
• Practise pronunciation.
• Play tape again. Students tick phrases.
• Check answers, whole class.

Asking for information
I'd like some information about...
Do you know...?
Could you tell me...?
Showing understanding
Right, I've got that.

Checking
Let me check.
I'll look that up.
Apologizing
I'm afraid I don't have any information about...
Asking for repetition
Could you repeat that, please?

10.5 🔲 **❸** Play tape. Students note down information.
• Students check information in pairs.
• Play tape again, if necessary.

Train times	**Paris**	**Bordeaux**
Wed arrive by 1 p.m.	10 a.m.	1 p.m.
Which station?	Paris Montparnasse	

10.5 🔲 **❹** Play tape again. Pause for students to complete questions.
• Check answers, whole class.
1 Can you tell me when you want to travel?
2 Could you tell me when it leaves?
3 Do you know which station it leaves from?

❺ Give students time to read examples and answer questions in pairs.
• Check answers, whole class.
An indirect question is more polite.
In an indirect question, there is no inversion of the subject and verb and no auxiliary verb
form, e.g. *do, does, did.*
• If explanation is needed, write sentence starters on board: *Could you tell me...?*
Do you know...? I'd like to know... and direct questions: *How far is it? What time
is it? Is it far? When does it leave? How long does it take?* Demonstrate with
arrows and erasure the changes of word order from question form to statement
form. Practise with prompt questions.

❻ Check answers, whole class.
1 and 3 are correct.
2 I'd like to know how long the journey takes.
4 Can you tell me which airport the flight leaves from?
5 Do you know how much the fare is?
6 I'd like to know where I can buy a ticket.
• Explain that it is not necessary or usual to use indirect questions repeatedly.
Follow-up activity Write on board: *Do you know...? Can you tell me...? Could you tell
me...?*
• Divide class into two groups, A and B.
• Students from both groups take turns to give the other group a direct question, which
that group has to change into an indirect question. The correct indirect question scores
a point.

❼ Students prepare questions in AA, BB pairs, then work in AB pairs for role-plays.
• Tell students to cover their partner's information.
• Students can sit back-to-back for the role-plays.
• After role-plays, students check each other's information.

Tapescript Unit 10

10.1 🔄

P=Presenter of radio programme, C1/C2/C3/C4=Callers to radio phone-in programme

P Good morning, and welcome to *Viewpoint*. Today's programme is about the problem of traffic congestion in our cities and on our roads. In the next twenty years the number of cars will double. Already traffic jams cost industry billions of dollars a year and there are 50,000 road deaths a year in Europe. What do you want the government to do about this problem? We're waiting for your calls. Call us now. Yes, we have our first caller on the line...

C1 Hello. Well, I'd like the government to spend money on improving public transport in cities. If we had a really good public transport system, we wouldn't need to use our own cars so much. We could park outside the city centre, and then use public transport inside the city. If we did that, we could all move around a lot more quickly.

P Right, so you think the answer is a better public transport system. Thank you, and let's hear from our second caller...

C2 Yes, well, I agree with the last caller, but good public transport costs a lot of money. I think we could make some of that money if we charged people for driving in cities. Make car drivers pay a fee! If motorists had to pay to drive in city centres, they would use their cars a lot less. And that would also mean fewer traffic jams.

P A good point, yes. Make drivers pay a fee. What do you think? Call us now. Ah, we have our third caller on the line... Hello?

C3 Well, I'm against building more and more motorways. This government thinks that if we had more motorways, we wouldn't have traffic jams on our roads, but that's just not true. More motorways mean more cars. If I were the Transport Minister, I would stop building motorways and spend the money on railways.

P Yes, I'm sure other listeners would agree with you on that. What does our fourth caller think? Hello?

C4 Good morning. Well, I would ban cars completely from city centres. If we didn't have all those cars, we wouldn't have all that pollution and noise. We need to think more about the people who live and work in cities, and their health. We want cities for people, not cities for cars.

P Right, thank you to those listeners. And now to discuss your ideas we have on our panel...

10.2 🔄

a. I'd do more sport if I had enough time.
b. If I earned more money, I'd buy a new car.

10.3 🔄

1 If I had a car, I'd drive it to work.
2 If I lived in the city, I'd travel by bike.
3 I'd take more exercise if I were you.
4 If they banned all cars, the air would be cleaner.
5 If the buses were quicker, more people would use them.
6 Would you take the train if you could?

10.4 🔄

R=Reservations clerk, BA Executive Club, C=Carol, Duncan Ross's secretary

R British Airways reservations. How can I help you?
C I'd like some information about flights from Edinburgh to Paris, on a Sunday afternoon, please.
R Certainly. Let me check. OK. There's one flight at 14.45, and two later flights at 16.00 and 18.00 hours. They all involve a transfer at Heathrow.
C What time does the first flight arrive?
R At 18.45.
C Could you repeat that, please?
R Certainly. 18.45.
C And when do the later flights arrive?
R The 16.00 gets in at 20.50, and the 18.00 at 23.05.
C Right, I've got that. Could you tell me the times of flights from Bordeaux to London, travelling on a Friday?
R I'll look that up. Right, there's just one British Airways flight daily, leaving at 14.40 and arriving at Gatwick at 15.10.
C Do you know if Air France flies from Bordeaux to London?
R I'm afraid I don't have any information about Air France flights. I can give you their telephone number.
C No, don't worry, I think the 14.40 flight will be fine. Thank you for the information. I'll get back to you later to book the flights.

10.5 🔄

F=Clerk at French Railways London office, C=Carol

F Good afternoon, French Railways.
C Good afternoon. I'd like to know the times of trains from Paris to Bordeaux.
F Can you tell me when you want to travel?
C Yes, on a Wednesday, arriving in Bordeaux by about 1 p.m.
F There's a TGV which arrives in Bordeaux at exactly 1 p.m.
C Oh, that's lucky. Could you tell me when it leaves?
F Yes, it leaves at 10 a.m.
C So the journey takes three hours?
F Yes, that's right.
C And do you know which station it leaves from?
F Yes, from Paris Montparnasse.
C Thank you. Oh, just one more question. Do I need to make a reservation?
F Yes, it's advisable.
C OK. I'll check with my boss, then phone you back. Thank you for your help.
F You're welcome.

UNIT 11

―― Notes ――――

Language focus   p. 98

Modal auxiliary verbs

1, 2   Quiz and discussion: social customs.
3, 4   Listening: social customs in different
       countries.   11.1 ▢▮
5   Identify verb forms in tapescript.
       Grammar analysis: modal auxiliary verbs.   (p. 13 📕)

Practice   p. 100

1   Matching exercise: modal verbs and meanings.
2   Sentence completion.
3   Advice to employees.
       Pronunciation: sentence meaning and
       shifting stress.   11.2, 11.3 ▢▮
4   Describe mini-culture of organization.
5   Group work: prepare advice for travellers.   (p. 66 📕)

Wordpower   p. 102

Personal characteristics

1   Matching exercise: personal characteristics.
2, 3   Using a dictionary to find opposites: practice.
4   Word building: suffixes.
5, 6   Describe qualities needed in jobs.   (11.1)
                                                 (p. 68 📕)

Skills focus   p. 103

Reading. Body language

1   Discussion and reading: cultural differences and
       body language.
2   Discuss article.
3, 4   Discussion: body language in different cultures.   (11.2)
5   Project: write a magazine article about body language.

Social English   p. 105

Social responses

1   Responses to common remarks.
2–5   Remarks and responses at a cocktail
       party.   11.4, 11.5 ▢▮
6   Role-play: social responses.
7, 8   Listen to check comments   11.6, 11.7 ▢▮
       and responses.   (p. 22 📕) (11.3)
                                                         (p. 70 📕)

The aim of the information in this unit is to raise awareness of cross-cultural differences, and of the misunderstandings that can occur through lack of awareness of those differences. The information is intended as a general guide to cultural behaviour in a country, not as a description of all the individuals in that country. While suggestions are made in these notes for group, pair, or whole class discussion, other groupings may be more appropriate for your particular class.

Language focus **1** Students tick statements individually.
- Students discuss answers in pairs. Ask students to be ready to report back to class on their partner's answers.
- Discuss answers, whole class. Encourage students to talk about their experiences.
- With mixed nationality classes, encourage students to ask each other questions about any differences they have noted. (This may be more appropriately done as pairwork with some groups.)

2 Give students time to think of examples of differences.
- Discuss questions, whole class.

11.1 **3** Students read through topics.
- Check vocabulary: *offend, good/bad manners, humorous, rude*
- Play each extract. Students tick topics.
- Students compare answers in pairs.

Topic	Extract 1	Extract 2	Extract 3
Shaking hands	✓		
First/family name	✓	✓	
Titles			✓
Business lunches	✓		
Punctuality		✓	
Humour and jokes		✓	
Business cards		✓	✓
Making decisions			✓
Invitations	✓	✓	✓

11.1 **4** Play tape again, if necessary. Students tick country.
- Students compare answers in pairs.
- Check answers, whole class.

Extract 1 France
Extract 2 Germany
Extract 3 Japan

5 Students work in pairs to find and underline verb forms, and discuss which form gives strongest advice.
- Check answers, whole class.

Must and *mustn't* offer the strongest advice.

Modal verbs
- Students read examples.
- Draw attention to the difference in meaning between *mustn't* and *needn't*.
- Students complete rules and answer questions in pairs.
- Check answers, whole class.

Use *should/shouldn't* to give advice.
Use *mustn't* to express a necessity not to do something.
Use *needn't* to express no necessity to do something.
Use *may* and *might* to express possibility.
Use modal verbs without *to* before the infinitive.
To make the negative, add *not* (-*n't*) to the end of modal verbs.

Refer students to Pocket Book p. 13.

Practice ❶ Students match modal verbs and definitions in pairs.
- Check answers, whole class.

A	B
must	it's 100% necessary
mustn't	it's 100% necessary not to do it
needn't	it's not necessary
should	it's a good idea
shouldn't	it's a bad idea
may	it's about 50% possible
might	it's less than 50% possible

Follow-up activity At this stage, or for review later, students test each other in pairs. One student reads the definition, and the other gives the modal verb.

❷ Tell students these sentences are based on information from the listening text.
- Students complete sentences individually.
- Check answers, whole class.

1 may/might   3 should   5 mustn't   7 needn't
2 must   4 may/might   6 shouldn't

❸ Students work in pairs to make sentences for each prompt. They can choose to make suggestions for a specific company, or for any company in general.
- Whole class feedback on their suggestions.

Pronunciation   This pronunciation practice is designed to demonstrate that where stress is placed in a sentence can affect meaning.

11.2 ① Play tape once. Students underline main stress in each sentence.
a. mustn't   b. papers
- To help students think about the change in meanings, prompt with questions: *How would you continue sentence a.? And b.?*

11.3 ② Play tape. Students underline stressed words.
1 You <u>might</u> need an umbrella.
2 You should take some <u>cash</u>.
3 You <u>must</u> wear a tie.
4 You <u>shouldn't</u> smoke in here.
5 You mustn't ask for <u>credit</u>.
6 You needn't do it <u>today</u>.

11.3 ③ Play tape again, pausing after each sentence to check answers to 2, and for students to repeat sentences.

④ Students work in pairs. Ask them to think how they could continue the sentences each time they change main stress. Ask them to keep a note of their ideas.
- Check suggestions, whole class.

---

❹ Students write lists individually, then compare their answers in pairs.
- Ask students to comment on any points from their partner's lists they found interesting/surprising.

❺ In mixed nationality classes, put students of the same nationality together, where possible. In classes of the same nationality, the topics can be divided among different groups.
- Monitor group work.
- Groups can present their advice to other groups, or write a short summary.

Wordpower ❶ Students complete table in pairs, checking vocabulary in dictionary, if necessary.
  • Check answers, whole class.

| 1 punctual | 3 sociable | 5 flexible | 7 patient | 9 agreeable |
| 2 polite | 4 honest | 6 sincere | 8 efficient | 10 ambitious |

  • Practise adjectives. Give description/definition and ask students to give the adjective.

❷ Check what prefixes students know. Prompt with questions: *What's the opposite of necessary? Possible? Employed?*
  • Write prefixes on board as they are mentioned.
  • Students complete the chart, using dictionary if necessary.

unpunctual   insincere   impolite   dishonest
unsociable   inflexible   impatient   disagreeable
unambitious

❸ Students prepare a description in writing, in pairs or individually.
  • Students read out descriptions, whole class.

❹ Students use dictionary to complete chart.
  • Check answers, whole class.

polite   politeness
ambitious   ambition
punctual   punctuality
efficient   efficiency
honest   honesty
patient   patience

Some suffixes are simply added, others involve changes in the adjective. Warn students to look carefully at spelling in their dictionaries.
  • Ask students to spell nouns. Write up on board.

❺ Students discuss points in pairs.

❻ Give students time to think about their answers.
  • Discuss question, whole class.

 Resource file 11.1

Skills focus ❶ Write *Body language* on the board. Ask students what they know about the topic, and what they would expect a text on it to include.
  • Check vocabulary: *gesture*
  • Students discuss questions in pairs, or as whole class.
  • Check vocabulary: *eye contact, fingertip, wrist, elbow*
  • Students read text and check their answers.

1 a. Italians, Greeks, Spanish, and Portuguese.   b. Swedes, Finns, Norwegians, and Danes.

2 North Europeans seem to need more personal space than south Europeans.

3 It seems to be more acceptable to stare at people in Mediterranean countries than in some other countries in Europe.

❷ Discuss question, whole class.

❸ Divide class into groups to discuss answers.
  • Discuss group findings, whole class.

❹ Discuss question, whole class. In single nationality groups, discuss any regional differences.

 Resource file 11.2

❺ Groups could brainstorm ideas/areas/topics to cover in articles, before individuals write.

Social English **1** Elicit possible answers, whole class.

⚷ (Possible answers)
1 It doesn't matter./Don't worry.
2 Don't mention it./Not at all.
3 Thanks, and the same to you.
4 Please do./ Well, I'd rather you didn't.
Do you mind if...? No = OK.

11.4 ◨ **2** Play tape. Students tick responses they think are appropriate.

11.5 ◨ **3** Play tape. Students check answers to 2.
⚷ 1 b.   2 a.   3 a.   4 b.   5 b.   6 a.   7 b.   8 a.
● Do whole class practice of the responses in 2 by giving prompts.

4 Ask students to keep a note of responses.
● Check suggestions, whole class.

5 Students work in pairs to match replies to comments and questions.
● Check answers, whole class.

⚷ 1 Can I get you another drink?   e. Thanks. I'll have a whisky.
2 Sorry, I've spilt some wine.   d. It doesn't matter.
3 Thank you for your all help.   f. Don't mention it.
4 You live in France, don't you?   c. Yes, that's right.
5 Do you mind if I smoke?   g. Well, I'd rather you didn't.
6 He's a millionaire, you know.   a. Really!
7 I lost the tennis match.   i. Never mind. Better luck next time.
8 May I join you?   b. Please do.
9 Could you pass the ice, please?   h. Yes, here you are.
10 Is this your first visit to Glencross?   j. No, I've been here before.

● Practise pronunciation of replies.
● Students practise in pairs. Student A reads comments, Student B responds. Then change.

6 Refer students to Pocket Book p. 22.
● Give students time to prepare a persona for the party, if appropriate.

11.6 ◨ **7** Play tape. Students tick responses, if appropriate.
⚷ 1 ✓   2 ✓   4 ✓   6 ✓   8 ✓

11.7 ◨ **8** Play tape. Students check answers.

RF   Resource file 11.3

Tapescript Unit 11

11.1
M=British manager giving a talk

Extract 1

M So, it's important to know about the differences in culture between your country and the country you're visiting or working in. If you don't know the social customs, you may make mistakes and offend people...

Handshaking is one example. In this country they shake hands much more than we do in the UK – every day, in fact, so you mustn't forget to do that. Another difference is that at work they use first names much less than we do in Britain, so call people by their family names. Food and wine are very important in this country, and at a business lunch you shouldn't start discussing business immediately. That might seem like bad manners. If you receive an invitation to a person's home, take good chocolates, flowers, or a good bottle of cognac. You shouldn't take wine because they drink that every day – it's too ordinary...

Extract 2

M Yes, for example in Britain, we often arrive five or ten minutes late for a meeting but in this country you should arrive on time, because people are normally very punctual in work situations. They usually arrive at the arranged time or earlier.

Family names, not first names, are more common at work and people use titles – Doctor and Professor, and so on. So you must remember to do the same. Your colleague will tell you if he or she wants you to use their first name.

Another difference is that you shouldn't try to be humorous or make jokes with people you don't know very well, because it might make them feel uncomfortable. Business meetings are usually serious. It's normal to exchange business cards at a first meeting, but you needn't do this until the end of the meeting. For social invitations, flowers or chocolates are suitable gifts. And you should give an odd number of flowers, say, eleven or thirteen, not twelve, and present them without the wrapping paper...

Extract 3

M So, when you go to this country, you should take plenty of business cards with you. They usually exchange cards at the beginning of a meeting, and they always read your card very carefully. You should do the same with theirs. They might think it rude if you don't.

In general, it takes longer to make decisions in this country than it does in Britain, so if you want to succeed, you must learn to be patient. And remember that when they say 'Yes', they may mean 'I understand', not 'I agree'. That often causes misunderstandings.

And a final piece of advice, it's not common, but if you receive an invitation to a person's home, you mustn't forget to take off your shoes before going inside, so make sure you're wearing clean socks!

11.2
a. You <u>mustn't</u> lose those papers.
b. You mustn't lose those <u>papers</u>.

11.3
Example   You shouldn't do it here.
                 You shouldn't do it here.
1   You might need an umbrella.
2   You should take some cash.
3   You must wear a tie.
4   You shouldn't smoke in here.
5   You mustn't ask for credit.
6   You needn't do it today.

11.4
1   I'm sorry. I didn't catch your name.
2   How about a drink?
3   You're from Spain, aren't you?
4   Sorry I'm late.
5   Can I get you something to eat?
6   We've got a lot of problems at the moment.
7   Thanks very much for your help.
8   Have a good weekend.

11.5
1   I'm sorry. I didn't catch your name.
     It's Simon. Simon Grant.
2   How about a drink?
     Not at the moment, thanks.
3   You're from Spain, aren't you?
     Yes, that's right.
4   Sorry I'm late.
     Don't worry.
5   Can I get you something to eat?
     Thank you. That would be very nice.
6   We've got a lot of problems at the moment.
     Oh, I'm sorry to hear that.
7   Thanks very much for your help.
     Not at all.
8   Have a good weekend.
     Thanks, the same to you.

11.6
1   May I use your phone?
2   Have a good holiday.
3   Could I ask you something?
4   I'm sorry, I've got the wrong number.
5   Thanks for the lovely flowers.
6   Someone stole my car last night.
7   Do you mind if I join you?
8   I'm getting married tomorrow.

11.7
1   May I use your phone?
     Yes, of course.
2   Have a good holiday.
     Thanks. You, too.
3   Could I ask you something?
     Yes, go ahead.
4   I'm sorry, I've got the wrong number.
     Don't worry.
5   Thanks for the lovely flowers.
     Don't mention it.
6   Someone stole my car last night.
     I'm sorry to hear that.
7   Do you mind if I join you?
     Not at all.
8   I'm getting married tomorrow.
     Congratulations.

UNIT 12

Language focus   p. 106

Passives: Present Simple, Past Simple, and Present
Perfect Simple

1   Discussion: champagne.
2   Reading: champagne making. Answer questionnaire.
3   Identify verb forms in text.
     Grammar analysis: Passives.   p. 14 PB

Practice   p. 108

1   Gap-fill: process description.
2   Make questions from text.   12.1 RF
3   Gap-fill: historical facts.
4   Pairwork information exchange: fact sheet.   12.2 RF
                                                      p. 72 WB

Wordpower   p. 112

Business headlines

1   Headlines vocabulary.
2   Word families: complete table.
     Pronunciation: stress in 3, 4, and
     5 syllable words.   12.1, 12.2
3   Pairwork: write headlines.

Skills focus   p. 113

Listening. Economic trends: markets and recession

1   Read and discuss headlines.
2   Interview with a consultant about the
     champagne market: complete notes.   12.3
3   Group work: prepare and give presentation from
     product information.
4   Project: prepare and give presentation on export facts
     and figures.

Social English   p. 115

Thanking and saying goodbye

1, 2 Leave-taking after a visit.   12.4
3   Role-play: thanks and responses.
4   Matching exercise: situations and responses.
5   Role-play: leave-taking and goodbyes.   p. 23 PB   12.3 RF
                                                      p. 77 WB

French terms such as *méthode champenoise, remuage, dégorgement,* are used in this unit, as they are the terms normally used in English.

Language focus ❶ Check vocabulary: *to deserve, defeat.* Ask students if they agree with this statement. Discuss question, whole class.

🔑 Napoleon said 'In victory you deserve it. In defeat you need it.'

❷ Check vocabulary from texts: *label, still (wine), sparkling (wine), cellars, to blend*
  • Students read the article and find the answers to the questionnaire.
  • Students compare answers in pairs.
  • Check answers, whole class.

🔑 1 Only sparkling wine which is produced in the Champagne area of France.
  2 The region is 'la Champagne'. The wine is 'le champagne'.
  3 No, it's made from two varieties of black grape, Pinot Noir and Pinot Meunier, and one white grape, Chardonnay. 'Blanc de Blancs' champagne is made from white grapes only.
  4 200 kilometres of chalk cellars.
  5 The Benedictine monk who developed the 'méthode champenoise' in the 17th century.
  6 Vintage champagne is produced from the grapes of the same year. Non-vintage champagne is made by blending the wine reserves of different years.

  • Ask students if any of the information surprised them.

❸ Make sure students look for only one example in each paragraph.
  • Students underline examples individually.
  • Students compare the examples they found, and discuss which tense verbs are, in pairs.

🔑 (Possible answers)
  is produced (Present Simple)   was made (Past Simple)   are used (Present Simple)
  have been used (Present Perfect Simple)   has been produced (Present Perfect Simple)

The Passive
  • Students read examples and complete rules in pairs.
  • Check answers, whole class.
  • Students answer questions in pairs.
  • Check answers, whole class.

🔑 To make the passive, use the verb *to be* in the correct tense + the past participle of the verb (e.g. *made, produced, grown*).
Use the passive when you want to describe actions without describing who does them.
When we want to say who does the action in a passive sentence, we use the word *by.*
  • Use the example sentences to point out that the choice of active or passive involves a change of emphasis.

Refer students to Pocket Book p. 14 and p. 16 (irregular verb list).

Practice ❶ Check vocabulary: *sediment, to ferment, to mature (Remuage* and *dégorgement* are defined in Practice 1 text.)
The pictures show the process of harvesting, levelling, racking, remuage, and labelling.
  • Students complete the text individually.
  • Check answers, whole class. Check vocabulary if necessary.

🔑 1 are picked   6 are blended   11 is removed   16 are added
  2 are used   7 are added   12 is carried out   17 is left
  3 are pressed   8 is bottled   13 are turned   18 are labelled
  4 are used   9 are produced   14 is frozen   19 are inserted
  5 is left   10 is produced   15 is removed   20 is sold

  • Draw attention to the use of the Present Simple Passive for describing a process. Prompt through questions: *What tense is this? What does it describe? So, which tense would you use to describe (how paper is made/a procedure in your office)?*

2 Students refer to the text in Language focus p. 106 for information.
- Check answers, whole class.

(Possible questions)
1 How long have vines been grown in the Champagne area of France?
2 When was champagne first made?
3 What is champagne made from?
4 How is 'Blanc de Blancs' champagne made?
5 How long have the chalk cellars been used?
6 How many days of sun are needed for a vintage year?
7 How is non-vintage champagne made?

Follow-up activity Divide class into two groups.
- Give groups time to write six questions in the passive about champagne. The answers must be in the Language focus or Practice 1 texts. Students should refer to the texts to prepare questions.
- Monitor preparation of questions.
- Groups exchange questions.
- Groups write answers to questions, referring to information in texts if necessary, and give back answers.
- Groups check answers to their questions. Award one mark each for correct language and correct information.

Resource file 12.1

3 Students complete text individually. Tell them to pay careful attention to tenses.
- Check answers, whole class.

1 has been exported	4 was solved	7 were hit	10 is called
2 was sold	5 was introduced	8 was imported	
3 were lost	6 was produced	9 is sold	

4 Find out what students already know about coffee production. Prompt with questions: *Where is it produced? How much is consumed?* etc.
- Check vocabulary: *exportable, to consume/consumption, per capita, per annum*
- Students work in AA, BB pairs to prepare their questions.
- Students work in AB pairs to complete their factsheets. Encourage them not to read each other's information.
- Check answers, whole class.

Resource file 12.2

Wordpower **1** Ask students if they read English newspapers and if so, whether they find headlines difficult to understand. Why?
- Students answer questions in pairs, using a dictionary if necessary.
- Check answers, whole class.

1 slump, recession
2 decade
3 boom
4 No. In the first headline *cut* is a verb. In the second, *cuts* is a noun.
5 Yes, it's good for export markets.
6 No. People are buying more.

Newspaper headlines in English have particular vocabulary conventions and often have different grammar from other written English. Auxiliaries and articles are usually omitted, and tenses tend to be simplified. Past participles can indicate Past Simple or Present Perfect, active or passive. The Present Simple is often used to describe what has happened or is happening, and the infinitive is usually used to refer to the future.

2 Students complete table individually.
- Check answers, whole class.

Verb	Noun (activity)	Noun (person)
compete	competition	competitor
consume	consumption	consumer
export	exporting	exporter
manufacture	manufacturing	manufacturer
produce	production	producer
recover	recovery	

Pronunciation
12.1 🔲 ① Play tape. Let students listen so that they can hear the different stress patterns.
- Students repeat words.

② Students work in pairs to put words in correct columns.

12.2 🔲 ③ Play tape. Students check answers.
⚷ consumption: fin<u>a</u>ncial, dom<u>e</u>stic
recovery: Austr<u>a</u>lian, appr<u>e</u>ciate
m<u>a</u>rketing: p<u>a</u>ssenger, tr<u>a</u>veller
competition: occup<u>a</u>tion, invit<u>a</u>tion

12.2 🔲 ④ Play tape again, pausing for students to repeat words.

⑤ Students work in pairs to mark stress pattern.
- Check answers, whole class.
⚷ pronunci<u>a</u>tion   celebr<u>a</u>tion   m<u>a</u>nager   pr<u>o</u>grammer
exped<u>i</u>tion   exhib<u>i</u>tion   corpor<u>a</u>tion   comp<u>u</u>ter

❸ Students work in pairs to write headlines.
- After pairs have written the first sentence of the article, pass it back to the original pair for comment.
Follow-up activity Students choose one headline and write whole article as homework.
Or Chain article. Pass articles round group, with each pair adding a sentence until there is a natural conclusion.

Skills focus ❶ Check vocabulary: *bubbly*, *fizz*
Two of these headlines show the tendency to use puns and alliteration in headlines.
- Discuss questions, whole class.

12.3 🔲 ❷ Give students time to read through James Turner's notes for the interview.
- Play the tape once. Students note down information.
- Students compare their initial answers in pairs.
- Play tape again. Students complete notes.
- Check answers, whole class. Play tape again, if necessary.
⚷ 1 **1980s – 'boom years'**

	Year	No. of bottles
Highest sales	1989	249 million
Highest production level	1990	293 million

2 **Decline in market since 80s**
Main reasons
1 the recession in champagne's export markets
2 the very high price of champagne
3 there was a lot of 'bad' champagne on the market

3 **Price of grapes (per kilo)**	**Today** 20 French francs	**In 1990** 36 French francs

4 **Market in future**
Increase in sales?   Yes, when economic situation improves.
Aim of changes   To make sure producers meet very high standards.

❸ Divide class into small groups. Allocate information A or B to each group.
- Groups can divide their presentation into parts, and each be responsible for one part, or appoint a spokesperson to give whole presentation.

❹ Agree a time limit for the presentation before students begin preparation.

Social English ❶ Remind students about the *Wine and Dine* celebration at Duncan's castle, Glencross.
- Elicit phrases students know for thanking people for hospitality. Prompt with questions: *What do you say when you are leaving a party? When you have had dinner at a friend's house?*
- Give students time to read questions for Dialogues 1–3.

12.4 ▢ • Play tape. Pause after each dialogue and check answers, whole class.

Dialogue 1
1 To stay with them in Bordeaux.
2 Yes, he has.

Dialogue 2
1 To stay at Glencross Castle again.
2 In London on the 22nd.

Dialogue 3
1 Another book.
(Possible answers)
2 Because he thinks their meeting is social or romantic.
3 Because other men find Monique attractive.

12.4 ▢ ❷ Students read through phrases.
- Practise pronunciation.
- Play tape again. Students tick phrases they hear.
- Check answers, whole class.

Thanking for hospitality
Thank you for inviting us.
Thank you very much for your hospitality.
Thanks a lot.

Responding to thanks
I'm glad you enjoyed it.

Saying goodbye
We really must leave now...
I must be off.
I'm looking forward to...
See you next week.
Have a good flight.
See you ... on the... next week...

Positive comment
We've had a wonderful time.
I really appreciated it.
Everything was great.

❸ Monitor pairwork.
- Check pairwork, whole class.

❹ Students match situations and responses individually.
- Check answers, whole class.
1 d.   2 c.   3 a.   4 b.

Follow-up activity In pairs, Student A chooses a situation from exercise 3 and 4. Student B makes an appropriate response. Then change.

❺ Students walk round class, giving real or fictional reason for leaving. Take a role yourself.

 Resource file 12.3

Tapescript Unit 12

12.1 🔲
a. consumption
b. recovery
c. marketing
d. competition

12.2 🔲
Australian
domestic
invitation
traveller
financial
occupation
passenger
appreciate

12.3 🔲
J=James Turner, F=Freddy Price
J Mr Price, what changes have you seen in the champagne market in the last ten to fifteen years?
F Well, the biggest change has been the decrease in sales since the great 'boom' years of the 1980s, when champagne production and sales reached record levels.
J Which was the best year?
F Well, the record was in 1989, when 249 million bottles of champagne were sold. The highest production level was reached in 1990, with a total of 293 million bottles. Of course, since those boom years sales have fallen.
J Has the market been badly hit by the recession?
F Oh, certainly. The economic problems in champagne's export markets – that's Europe, the United States, Japan, and of course the domestic market in France – the economic problems have certainly been one reason for the decrease in champagne sales.
J And the other reasons?
F Another important factor has been price. In the early 90s, champagne was very over-priced, so many people stopped buying it. Instead they bought sparkling wines from other countries – in particular from Australia, California, and Spain. And then, there was another problem for champagne in the early nineties.
J What was that?
F There was a lot of rather bad champagne on the market. This meant the popularity of good sparkling wines increased even more. People were surprised by their quality and, of course, they were a lot cheaper than champagne.
J Have champagne producers been forced to reduce their prices because of this competition?
F Well, champagne prices have come down since the early 90s, but I think this is more because of the reduction in the price of grapes than because of the competition from sparkling wines. Today the price of grapes is around 20 French francs a kilo – a lot more realistic than the 1990 price of about 36 francs a kilo.
J Do you think the champagne market will recover in the future?
F Oh, I'm sure it will. When the economic situation improves, I believe the market will recover. Recently some important changes have been introduced. The aim is to make sure the producers meet very high standards and produce the best quality. I think these changes will produce very good results.
J So, that's good news for the consumers of those 200 million bottles a year?
F Yes, certainly. In fact, good news for all of us.

12.4 🔲
P=Pierre, D=Duncan, A=Anne-Marie, M=Monique, J=James
Dialogue 1
P Duncan, we really must leave now or we'll miss our plane back to Bordeaux. Thank you for inviting us, we've had a wonderful time.
D I'm glad you enjoyed it, Pierre. And thank you for inviting me to stay with you. I'm really looking forward to it.
A And so are we. Goodbye, Duncan. See you next week in Bordeaux.
D Goodbye, Anne-Marie, Pierre. Have a good flight.

Dialogue 2
M Duncan, thank you very much for your hospitality. I really appreciated it.
D Well, I'm very pleased you agreed to stay a few more days. You must come and stay whenever you like, Monique.
M Thank you, I promise I will. So, goodbye, Duncan. See you in London on the 22nd.
D Yes, I'll ring you next week to fix the time. Goodbye, Monique.

Dialogue 3
D Well, James, thanks for all your help organizing the *Wine and Dine* celebration, and congratulations – everybody was very impressed by your book! I think you should write another one!
J Yes, I'll think about it. Er, Duncan, you're meeting Monique in London on the 22nd?
D Yes. To discuss the French edition of *Wine and Dine*. Monique has agreed to do all the translation work.
J Oh, good, I thought… well…
D Don't worry, James, it's strictly business. Although I must say Monique's a very attractive and interesting person!
J Yes, I know, that's the problem. Well, I must be off. I'm driving Monique to the airport. Thanks a lot, Duncan. Everything was great.
D Bye, James, and don't forget to think about that second book, not just your social life! Bye, James. (*shouts*) Bye, Monique.

Review units

Each Review unit aims to review all the grammar and Social English exponents from the previous four units. There is also an exercise designed to encourage students to check vocabulary. The Review units are intended to be used in class; the Resource file has corresponding tests.

The review exercises are designed to be independent of each other. Encourage students to decide for themselves what they need to review further, by using the self-check box at the end. Each unit has a variety of pairwork and group work exercises, and a standard format, so that students can work through the unit with minimum intervention from the teacher.

Method 1

- At the end of the previous class, tell students there will be a review session in the next lesson. Ask them to revise the work from the previous units.
- In class, students work through the Grammar exercises in pairs, following the instructions for each one. Encourage students to use the Pocket Book for reference, and to ask you for help, as they work through.
- Check answers, whole class.
- Students change pairs and work through Social English exercises.
- Monitor students' work.
- Check answers, whole class.
- Give brief feedback session on any points that came up during monitoring.
- Students change pairs and practise Social English exercises again, if necessary.
- Divide students into groups to prepare and do Vocabulary test.
- Students read and mark the self-check box.
- Agree a time when students will do the corresponding test.

Method 2

- At the end of the previous class, tell students there will be a review session in the next lesson. Ask them to revise the work from the previous units.
- In class, ask students to read the headings for each Grammar exercise in the unit, and to decide which they need to work on.
- Allocate students into pairs who want to practise similar areas.
- Students work through Grammar exercises, following the instructions for each one. Monitor, and answer questions, etc.
- Follow same procedure for Social English exercises.
- Divide students into groups to prepare and do Vocabulary test.
- Students read and mark the self-check box.
- Agree a time when students will do the corresponding test.

 Test A p. 164, Test B p. 166, Test C p.168

Review unit A: answers

3 speak English on the phone, play a sport, write letters in English, make business trips, give presentations, work flexitime, read professional literature, attend meetings or conferences

4

1 writes	6 is doing	11 flew	16 enjoyed	21 likes
2 moved	7 is visiting	12 spent	17 didn't like	
3 lives	8 specialize	13 was	18 loves	
4 isn't	9 is interviewing	14 joined	19 meets	
5 spends	10 have	15 talked	20 does she enjoy	

5 (Possible questions)

1 Where did you go?
2 How long did you go for?
3 Was it your first holiday in Majorca?
4 Where did you stay?

5 Did you like the Spanish food?
6 What did you do?
7 What was the weather like?
8 Did you have any problems?

6
1 fewer, fewest
2 livelier, liveliest
3 more crowded, most crowded
4 better, best
5 more suitable, most suitable
6 more, most

7 farther (further), farthest (furthest)
8 worse, the worst
9 more enjoyable, most enjoyable
10 less, least
11 bigger, biggest
12 easier, easiest

9 (Possible answers)

Could I speak to
's calling
This is
the line

isn't here
take a message?
Could you ask him
I'll give him your message

1 2, 3, 5, 6, and 9 are correct.
1 Could you give me some information, please?
4 He gave me some useful advice.
7 How much money did you spend?
8 I haven't got any paper.
10 He has a lot of experience in marketing.

3

Student A	**Student B**
1 Have you ever been...?	1 Have you ever been...?
2 Have you ever had...?	2 Have you ever had...?
3 Have you ever missed...?	3 Have you ever studied or worked...?
4 Have you ever worked...?	4 Have you ever met...?
5 Have you ever lost...?	5 Have you ever wanted...?

4
1 I haven't seen him for ages.
2 How long ago did you have a holiday?
3 How long have they been married?
4 I've had my present job for a long time.
5 Have you ever been to Canada?
6 How many candidates have you interviewed today?
7 She changed her job a month ago.
8 How long have you been working for your present company?
9 He changed jobs twice last year.
10 She's studied Japanese since 1993.

5
1 has been	4 has worked	7 went	10 is	13 have visited
2 left	5 travels	8 hasn't been	11 have never visited	
3 joined	6 was	9 is	12 flew	

6
| 1 You've drunk | 3 She's typed, I've signed | 5 They've been walking |
| 2 We've been drinking | 4 He's played | 6 She's lost, She's been looking |

3 1 mustn't   2 must   3 needn't   4 mustn't   5 must   6 needn't

4 1 h.   2 e.   3 f.   4 a.   5 g.   6 b.   7 c.   8 d.

6
1 was introduced	4 was drunk	7 has been developed
2 was added	5 was opened	8 is consumed
3 was made	6 has been produced	9 is eaten

8
1 Could you tell me what the plane fare from Barcelona to Paris is?
2 Do you know how long the flight takes?
3 Can you tell me which airport in Paris the plane arrives at?
4 Could you tell me when I need to check in?
5 Do you know if I can buy duty-free goods on the plane?

9 1 c.   2 e.   3 f.   4 g.   5 h.   6 a.   7 b.   8 d.

Resource file and Index

Index
The index gives details of the file type, the language point being practised, and indicates the first point at which the material can be used.

Instructions
Instructions are provided for the card and grammar practice activities, but many of the materials in the Resource file need no instructions; information to enable students to carry out the tasks is given on the photocopiable sheet. Those activities which have instructions are marked ● in the index.

Grammar file
The Grammar file provides activities based on the 'discovery' approach to teaching grammar used in the Student's Book, and which relate to the target grammar of each unit. All activities require students to analyse data and think about grammatical form and meaning.

There are grammar games with cards; concept cards which develop students' understanding of grammatical concept and use through analysis of examples, and practice cards which provide opportunities to put this knowledge to use. The activities are played as games, to change the focus of the lesson, and to provide opportunities for students to check their understanding of the grammatical concepts they have been studying. To make the cards, cut up the photocopied sheets, stick each 'paper card' onto strong card and cover each card with adhesive film. It is worth spending the time producing sets of cards in this way as they will last much longer.

Vocabulary file
The Vocabulary file provides material for regular and systematic reviews of the key vocabulary in the Student's Book, and for vocabulary extension work.

Skills file
The Skills file has a variety of activities including role-play, discussion, and games, which extend the topics in the Student's Book and give students further practice in speaking, reading, and writing. There are also texts and information transfer activities, based on authentic sources, which provide further vocabulary and skills work, with communicative tasks which require students to read, understand, and exchange information.

Social file
This file provides activities which review the functional language taught in the Social English section of the Student's Book.

Writing file
The activities in this file are designed in particular for students who want further practice in corresponding in English, and are designed to be used as communication practice activities in class.

Situations file
This material gives students useful vocabulary and functional language for coping with some of the common situations and problems they may meet, and covers situations not dealt with in the Student's Book.

Tests
These can be used after Units 4, 8, and 12.

Answer key
This is photocopiable, to give students the opportunity to check their own work. Activities which have answers are marked ▲ in the index.

FILE	LANGUAGE POINT FOCUS/TOPIC	TITLE	USE
1.1● Grammar	Present Simple and question words	Find someone who...	Practice 4 p. 4
1.2● Grammar	Present Simple	Grammar cards	Practice 4 p. 4
1.3 Vocabulary	Learning vocabulary	How to learn vocabulary	Wordpower 4 p. 7
1.4 Vocabulary	British/American English ▲	British and American English: What's the difference?	Skills focus 3 p. 8
1.5 Social	Introductions and greetings	Introductions and greetings	Social English 5 p. 9
1.6 Vocabulary	Vocabulary review ▲	Vocabulary review and extension	after Unit 1
2.1● Grammar	Present Simple, Continuous ▲	Grammar cards	Practice 2 p. 11
2.2● Grammar	Present Simple, Present Continuous, frequency adverbs ▲	What's the mistake?	Practice 2 p. 11
2.3 Skills	Language for presentations	Presentations	Skills focus 3 p. 15
2.4 Skills	Numbers, Present Simple	Vinexpo – the centre of the wine world	Skills focus 4 p. 15
2.5 Skills	Telling the time	What's the time?	Social English 10 p. 17

Index

Instructions

1.1, 3.2, 8.1
- Give each student a copy of the question sheet.
- Students move round the class, asking each other questions. As soon as they '*find someone who…*', they write the name in the space, then ask appropriate follow-up questions. They then move on to question another student.
- At the end of the activity, students report back on selected items.

1.2 These are prompt cards which can be used for whole-class practice or by students working in groups.

Method 1
- Enlarge cards for use as flash cards with whole class.
- Use for question-answer practice. Give prompts, e.g. *Ask Do you…? Ask How often…? Ask When…?*. Students make questions, others answer, across class.

Method 2
- Demonstrate use of cards, as above.
- Divide students into groups.
- Give each group a set of cards, face down in a pile.
- Students pick up cards in turn and use as prompts for question-answer practice.

2.1 These cards are used for matching grammar concepts with sample exponents.

- Divide students into groups.
- Give each group a set of concept cards (*routine activities* etc.), and a set of exponents cards (*I sometimes visit trade fairs* etc.).
- Students match exponents with concepts.
- Check answers, whole class.
- Students write two more examples for each category of the concept cards.

2.2, 3.1, 7.2 *What's the mistake?* worksheets focus on grammar errors which have been selected to highlight general problem areas. You may also like to make your own 'mistake' sheets, to focus on your students' particular problem areas. See also the monitor sheet (Resource file p. 163).

- Give each student a copy of the worksheet. Explain that each sentence contains one error only.
- Students work individually or in pairs to find errors and correct sentences.
- Check answers, whole class.

4.1
- Check vocabulary of adjective cards.
- Divide students into groups.
- Give each group a set of adjective cards, face down in a pile. Place the six topic cards on table, face up.
- In turn, students pick up an adjective card and choose one of the six topics. They make a comparison (of cities, sports, etc.) using the comparative or superlative form of the adjective.
- Groups select six of their most interesting comparisons, and write them down. They then read them out to the rest of the class.

5.1 **Stage 1**
- Divide students into groups.
- Give each group a set of the three headings cards (mass, count, mass and count), and a set of noun cards.
- Students match noun cards with headings cards.

Stage 2
- Give each group the *some/any*, etc. cards, face down in a pile.
- In turn students pick up a card, and make a sentence with an appropriate noun.
- Students write a sentence for each *some/any*, etc. card, then refer to Pocket Book p. 6 to check they are correct.

6.3
- Students work in pairs. Give each pair a dice, 2 counters, 1 board, and a set of question cards.
- Students shuffle question cards, and place them face down.
- Students throw dice to move round board. When they land on a ? square, their partner takes a question from the pile and asks the question; they answer.

7.1
- Divide students into groups.
- Give each group the two concept cards and a set of exponents cards.
- Students match the exponents with concept cards.
- Students match pairs of exponents cards.
- Check answers, whole class.
- Check use of Past Simple and time expressions for past situations and actions, and Present Perfect Simple for past to present situations, and use of *for* and *since*.
- Students write two more examples for each concept card.

9.1 **Stage 1**
- Check vocabulary of concept cards (*Definite Situations* etc.).
- Divide students into groups.
- Give each group a set of concept cards and a set of exponents cards (*I think ...* etc.).
- Students match exponents with headings.

Stage 2
- Give each group a set of predictions cards, face down in a pile.
- In turn students pick up a card and read out the prediction.
- Each student in group gives his/her opinion using one of the phrases on the exponents cards. Students discuss their opinions and agree or disagree. Refer Students to Pocket Book p. 20, Opinions.
- Groups write down four predictions of their own, and give them to another group to discuss in the same way.
- Whole class feedback on some of the predictions.

9.2
- Divide students into groups.
- Give each group a set of headings cards, and a set of practice cards, the latter face down in a pile.
- In turn students pick up a practice card and decide the type of future the phrase on the card suggests (arrangement, plan, prediction, etc.).
- Student asks the others in their group questions, using the phrase on the card with an appropriate future form.
- Student places card under appropriate heading. If more than one heading is possible, tell students to select one.
- Students write two questions for each future form (*going to, will,* Present Continuous) and give to another group to answer.
- Whole class feedback on some of the questions.

11.3
- Divide students into pairs or small groups.
- Give each group two sets of cards, shuffled. Make sure students realize that response cards can go with more than one card.
- Students match cards.
- Students turn the response cards face down, and practise responses without reading.

Monitor sheet   This aims to encourage learner independence, to encourage students to correct themselves, and to provide revision/remedial work.

A monitor sheet can be used during an individual student presentation, or at any time when you choose to focus on one student's performance, or to note 'collective' problems during a lesson/activity. Be selective about errors noted, and make sure that students keep monitor sheets for reference.

Method 1

- Use the monitor sheet to note down mistakes, and the symbols to indicate the nature of the mistake. Do not write the correction.
- Give the student the sheet. When he/she has corrected as many points as he/she can, go through the rest of the sheet and supply any further corrections.
- Encourage the student to check the sheet at a later date, to see whether the corrections are still clear.

Method 2

- Use the monitor sheet to note down mistakes, and the symbols to indicate the nature of the mistake. Do not write the correction. You may choose to note a student name if you want him/her to focus on a particular point, but in general mistakes should be anonymous.
- Copy the sheet for the class, or write on board.
- Students work individually, in pairs, or in small groups to correct errors.
- Check answers, whole class.
- Review the sheet at a later stage in the course. For example, elicit corrections orally, or use a compilation of mistakes from a number of sessions for pairwork correction, as a warmer or filler activity.

Find someone who...

	Name
speaks two or more foreign languages	
likes sport	
walks to work	
goes skiing	
makes a lot of business trips	
has a pet	
attends conferences	
speaks English every day	
has an unusual hobby or leisure activity	
enjoys photography	

Ask your colleagues questions with *When*, *Where*, *How often*, *What*, or *How*, to get more information. Make notes of their answers.

Grammar cards

attend a meeting/conference 1.2	commute to work 1.2
make a business trip 1.2	give a presentation 1.2
enjoy photography/travel 1.2	play tennis/golf 1.2
go skiing/sailing 1.2	use a computer 1.2
speak English on the phone 1.2	drive to work 1.2
enjoy travelling/meeting people 1.2	read a newspaper 1.2

1.3 VOCABULARY FILE

How to learn vocabulary

Here are some suggestions to help you learn new vocabulary.
Choose the ways that are best for you.

What?
Don't try to learn every new word. Choose words you know you need.

Where?

1 **In a vocabulary notebook**

- Buy a special notebook for vocabulary.
- Decide how you want to organize the pages. Order them alphabetically (a.), by topic (b.), or by date (c.).

a.

F

fit = healthy. I do a lot of sport to keep fit.
failure = opposite of success
flight = journey by plane. Have a good flight!

b.

Jobs
accountant
doctor
stewardess
engineer

c.

Wednesday 4 October
Unit 1
vineyard = area where vines grow (for making wine)
salary = the money you get for working (monthly)
to live in the suburbs = outside the city centre

2 **On vocabulary cards**

- Buy some cards and keep them in a box.
- Write the new word on one side.
- Add useful information about the word.
- On the other side, write an explanation in English, or an example, or a translation, or draw a picture!

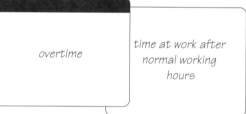

overtime

time at work after normal working hours

translator (person)
translation (thing)
to translate from ...
into ...

She's a translator. She translates documents from French into English.

Knife
fork
spoon

3 **On cassette**

- Record new vocabulary onto a cassette tape. Listen to it when you are driving, jogging or cooking the family meal!

When?

- Try to learn five to ten new words every day.
- Carry your vocabulary notebook or cards with you, and review vocabulary whenever you can.

What else?

- Read as much as possible in English, e.g. easy readers like *Oxford Bookworms*, newspapers, and magazines.
- Listen to English on the radio, e.g. BBC World Service, and watch TV programmes in English. Choose a topic you know. If you already know something about a topic in your own language, (e.g. a news item) it helps you to understand.

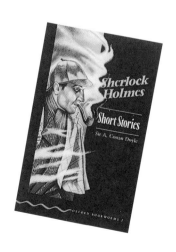

Good luck with your vocabulary learning!

British and American English: What's the difference?

1 Look at the examples of American English vocabulary. Find the British English words with the same meaning in the box and write them in the spaces.

Example   We always take our **vacation** in July.
            holiday

He lives in a very pleasant **apartment**.
....

Do you take the **subway** to work?
....

I need some shampoo from the **drugstore**.
....

Where's the **restroom**, please?
....

Take the **elevator** to the second floor.
....

I'd like a **round trip** ticket, please.
....

chemist's	lift	flat	return	toilet	underground

2 Match the American English words in Column A with the British English words in Column B.

A	B
cab	autumn
freeway	taxi
movie theater	cinema
fall	pavement
pants	motorway
sidewalk	trousers

3 There are some differences in British and American spelling. Write *American* or *British* in the headings below. Use your dictionary to complete the list.

.... English	.... English
cheque	....
....	color
....	theater
catalogue	....
....	program
traveller	....

4 Study the list above, then look at the letters underlined in the words below. What is the British spelling? Check the answer in your dictionary.

fav<u>o</u>rite	<u>l</u>iter	dia<u>log</u>	cen<u>ter</u>	lab<u>or</u>
....	....	....	....	....

Introductions and greetings

Answer the questions. Then discuss your answers with your partner.

	Yes	No	It depends
Introductions			
1 When I introduce myself, I usually give my first name and family name.			
2 I only shake hands with people when I meet them for the first time, or when I see them after a long time.			
3 In a professional situation, I always give the person I meet my business card.			
4 After an introduction, I try to use the person's name several times to remember it.			
5 I always keep eye contact with a person when I talk to them.			
6 I keep to 'safe' topics at first meetings.			

Greetings

How do these people usually greet each other in your culture?
Do they use first or family names?

- colleagues who see each other at work every day

- friends who often meet socially

- professional acquaintances who meet two or three times a year

Other cultures

How do people in other countries introduce and greet each other? Describe any differences you know.

Vocabulary review and extension

1 Read the clues, and fill in the spaces. All the words are in Unit 1.

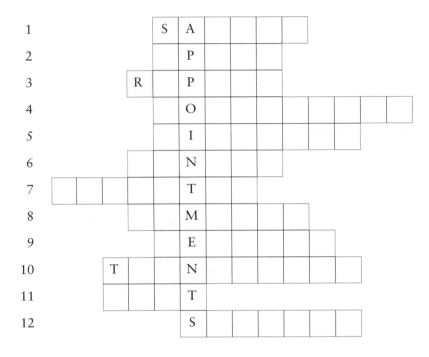

1 S A
2 P
3 R P
4 O
5 I
6 N
7 T
8 M
9 E
10 T N
11 T
12 S

1 the money you get for working
2 'Could you .... your name, please?'
3 'I'm sorry, I don't understand. Could you .... that, please?'
4 the people you work with
5 a piece of land where vines grow
6 'He's not married, he's ....'
7 'She has three children; two sons and a ....'
8 'I work in the city centre but I don't live there. I .... to work every day.'
9 free time, when you don't work
10 'Monique is a .... and interpreter.'
11 'I live in a .... on the third floor.'
12 'People who live in the .... usually go to work by car or train.'

2 Look at the pictures and fill in the spaces. The missing words are all sporting activities ending in *-ing*.

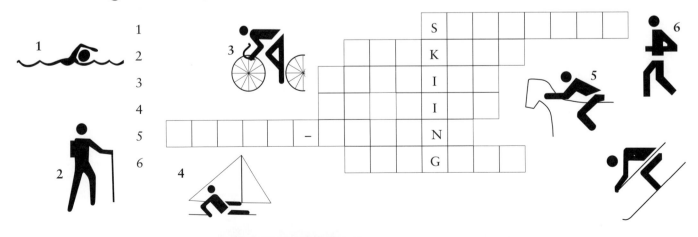

1 S
2 K
3 I
4 I
5 — N
6 G

Grammar cards

permanent or long-term situations 2.1	routine activities 2.1
activities happening at the time of speaking 2.1	temporary situations or events in progress 2.1

He works for an international company. 2.1	I'm taking the train to work this month. 2.1	Our company is entering new markets. 2.1
He's talking to a customer at the moment. 2.1	I usually play tennis at weekends. 2.1	I don't often make business trips abroad. 2.1
My journey to work takes about 45 minutes. 2.1	Competition in the airline industry is growing. 2.1	We export to France and Spain. 2.1
Mr Bell is having lunch with a customer. 2.1	The sales manager is making a presentation. 2.1	I sometimes visit trade fairs. 2.1

GRAMMAR FILE
What's the mistake?

Each of these sentences has a grammar mistake. Find the mistake, then write the correct sentence.

1 Peter is often making business trips to the USA.

....

2 When do you start usually work?

....

3 How often are you coming here?

....

4 He talks to a visitor at the moment.

....

5 I play never tennis in the winter.

....

6 I'm having four weeks' holiday every year.

....

7 He never is late.

....

8 We do a lot of extra work this week.

....

9 Currently our sales increase.

....

10 I travel always to work by car.

....

Presentations

The introduction

Today I'd like to | tell you about…

                 | talk to you about…

                 | present…

First, I'll speak about…

Then, …

Finally, …

Ordering the information

I'll begin with…

Now | I'll move on to…

      | I'll tell you about…

      | I'll describe…

Checking understanding

Is that clear?

Is that OK?

Referring to visuals

This | chart   shows…   As you can see from this | chart…

     | diagram | diagram…

Finishing

Thank you for listening.

Thank you for your attention.

Are there any questions?

Vinexpo - the centre of the wine world

INFORMATION SHEET 1   STUDENT A

You and your partner are journalists who want to go to Vinexpo. You both have some information about the exhibition, and a list of points you want to know.

1 Read your information about Vinexpo.

2 Prepare questions to ask your partner about the points in the box below.

3 Answer your partner's questions.

4 Ask your partner questions to find out the information you need.

Vinexpo –
the centre of the wine world

Vinexpo is the most important wine and spirits exhibition in the world. It takes place every two years in Bordeaux and lasts for five days. There are about 2,000 exhibitors. Sixty-five per cent of the exhibitors are French and the other thirty-five per cent come from 40 different countries. More than 55,000 people who work in the wine and spirits business visit Vinexpo, and they come from over 90 countries. The number of visitors and exhibitors increases each year.

There is a full programme every day. It includes seminars, presentations, competitions, discussions, and very important – wine tastings! As Vinexpo is a very important international event, there is a lot of interest from the media, so it is not surprising that the 55,000 visitors include more than 800 journalists, from all over the world.

Find out:

1 the distance from Bordeaux airport to Vinexpo.
2 the best way to get to Vinexpo.
3 the time the TGV (high-speed train) takes from Paris to Bordeaux.
4 how to get from Vinexpo to your hotel.
5 about car parking at Vinexpo.
6 who can visit Vinexpo.
7 where you can eat at Vinexpo.
8 where you can get more information.

Vinexpo - the centre of the wine world

INFORMATION SHEET 2 STUDENT B

You and your partner are journalists who want to go to Vinexpo. You both have some information about the exhibition, and a list of points you want to know.

1 Read your information about Vinexpo.

2 Prepare questions to ask your partner about the points in the box below.

3 Ask your partner questions to find out the information you need.

4 Answer your partner's questions.

Vinexpo –
the centre of the wine world

Vinexpo takes place at the Bordeaux-Lac Exhibition Centre, just ten minutes by bus from the city centre, the railway station, and Bordeaux airport.

TRANSPORTATION

There are flights to Bordeaux from thirty-eight cities in France and abroad. There are excellent train connections to other cities in Europe, and the train journey from Paris to Bordeaux takes only three hours by TGV.

There are shuttle bus connections between Vinexpo and the airport, the railway station, and hotels. Car parking at Vinexpo is free.

ADMISSION

Vinexpo is for people in the wine and spirits trade only. All visitors must have a badge with their name.

RESTAURANTS

The Exhibition Centre has several restaurants.

- The 'Restaurants du Lac' serve specialities from different countries and regions.
- Restaurants near the car park serve traditional French cuisine.
- New cafeterias inside Buildings 1 and 2 serve quick lunches.

SPECIAL SERVICES

- Computers, with general information about Vinexpo and answers to your questions.
- Information desks with trilingual hostesses.
- Hotel and airline reservations.
- International newpapers and magazines.
- Meeting point and message board.
- Medical assistance, post office, and bank.

Find out:

1 how often Vinexpo takes place.
2 how long it lasts.
3 how many exhibitors there are.
4 where exhibitors come from.
5 how many visitors there are.
6 where they come from.
7 how you can spend your time at Vinexpo.
8 if there are the same number of visitors as last time.

What's the time?

1 Look at these ways of saying the time.

`08:00` It's eight o'clock.

 It's half past nine. *or* It's nine thirty.

 It's eight a.m. *or* It's eight in the morning. `06:15` It's a quarter past six. *or* It's six fifteen.

`20:00` It's eight p.m. *or* It's eight in the evening. It's a quarter to eleven. *or* It's ten forty-five.

2 Work in pairs. What time is it? Ask and answer. Practise both ways.

  `04:45` `02:25`

Example   *What time is it?* Or
Can you tell me the time?

It's half past seven. Or
It's seven thirty.

3 Do not say minutes with five, ten, twenty, and twenty-five.

`12:10` It's ten past twelve. (not ten minutes past twelve.)

 It's twenty-five to four.

`11:07` It's seven minutes past eleven. (not seven past eleven.)

 It's twenty-one minutes to five.

4 Work in pairs. What time is it? Ask and answer.

5 Use the twenty-four hour clock for timetables and travel announcements.

Example   *The BA flight to Tokyo leaves at seventeen forty-five.*

Work in pairs. Student A cover Chart 2. Student B cover Chart 1. Ask questions to complete your chart.

Example   Student A   *What time does flight BA 442 leave?*
Student B   *At seventeen fifteen.*

Chart 1		
BA 246	Johannesburg	21.45
BA 418	Luxembourg	____
BA 031	Beijing	____
BA 808	Copenhagen	17.50
BA 952	Munich	13.15
BA 033	Kuala Lumpur	____

Chart 2		
BA 246	Johannesburg	____
BA 418	Luxembourg	19.20
BA 031	Beijing	15.35
BA 808	Copenhagen	____
BA 952	Munich	____
BA 033	Kuala Lumpur	18.25

6 Work in pairs. Make a class survey. *What time do you...?* Prepare 10 questions. Ask the rest of the class.

Vocabulary review

Read the clues, and fill in the spaces. All the words are in Unit 2.

1				H						
2				E						
3				A						
4		P		D						
5				Q						
6				U						
7				A						
8				R						
9	C			T						
10				E						
11				R						
12				S						

1 '.. the line, please.'

2 'I'm sorry, he's not here today. Can I take a ....?'

3 In my job I .... meetings every day.

4 What .... does your company make?

5 They make high .... cars.

6 30,000 .... spend about £1.5 million on an average day in Harrods.

7 The Swatch product .... includes watches, mobile phones, sunglasses, and mountain bikes.

8 Ikea's worldwide .... is 24 billion Swedish kronor.

9 This means 'at present'.

10 The company has 2,000 .... at present, and 200 more are starting work this month.

11 He's giving a .... of the new product to the sales team.

12 The shop gets its products from different ....

GRAMMAR FILE

What's the mistake?

Each of these sentences has a grammar mistake. Find the mistake, then write the correct sentence.

1 I didn't went on holiday last year.

....

2 When you bought your car?

....

3 Who did you met at the party?

....

4 How much did you paid for the ticket?

....

5 Stephen and Martyn came not to work yesterday.

....

6 When started you to play golf?

....

7 Why didn't you came on time?

....

8 Sales not increased last year.

....

9 What time he started work last week?

....

10 How often they visited you?

....

3.2 GRAMMAR FILE

Find someone who…

STUDENT A

	Name
played a sport yesterday	
went to bed after midnight last night	
read a newspaper this morning	
cooked dinner yesterday	
travelled abroad last summer	
had a birthday last month	
studied English last night	
drank wine yesterday lunchtime	

Ask follow-up questions to get more information.

3.2 # Find someone who…

STUDENT B

	Name
spoke English yesterday	
went to a restaurant yesterday	
made a business trip last month	
went skiing last winter	
watched the news on TV yesterday evening	
worked overtime last week	
attended a conference last year	
bought something new last month	

Ask follow-up questions to get more information.

Madame Tussaud's

1 Read the article about Madame Tussaud's. Use a dictionary if necessary.

2 Work in groups.

1 Write 10 questions about the text. Exchange your questions with another group.
2 Answer the questions as a group. Do not look at the article again. Give your answers back.
3 Check the other group's answers. Give one mark for the correct facts and one mark for correct English.

Madame Tussaud's

Madame Tussaud's is the most famous wax museum in the world and every year it attracts more than two and a half million visitors, which makes it one of London's most popular tourist attractions.

The life of its founder, Madame Tussaud, was extraordinary for a woman in the 19th century. She was born in 1761 in Strasbourg, France. She was called Marie Grosholtz then. Her father was a soldier who died in battle two months before her birth. She spent the first five years of her life in Berne, Switzerland, where her mother worked as a housekeeper to a doctor. Then the doctor moved to Paris, and Marie and her mother went with him.

The doctor was an expert in wax modelling and he taught Marie his skill. When she was seventeen, she made two wax models which are still in the exhibition today: one of the French philosopher, Voltaire, and the other of the American statesman, Benjamin Franklin. In 1780 the French court invited her to Versailles to teach art to the sister of the French king, Louis XVI. She worked at Versailles for nine years, until the French Revolution in 1789.

During the French Revolution Marie and her mother were in prison for several years. Then the regime freed them and ordered Marie to make death masks of many of her previous employers who died by the guillotine – including Louis XVI and his wife, Marie-Antoinette.

In 1794 the doctor died and Marie inherited his exhibition of wax models. A year later she married a French engineer, François Tussaud. They had three children: a daughter, who died, and two sons. In 1802 she decided to leave France and her husband and tour Britain with her exhibition.

During the next 33 years she visited all the major towns and cities in Britain and presented her exhibition. It was a sensational success. In 1835, tired of travelling and aged 74, she decided to establish a permanent exhibition in London.

She continued to run the exhibition until her death in 1850, at the age of 89. Her two sons inherited the exhibition and in 1884, Madame Tussaud's moved to its present location in Marylebone Road, London.

Useful language	
When was she born?	She was born in…
What did he do? What was her name?	He worked as a… She was called…
How old was he when…?	He was seventeen (years old), when… At the age of… Until his death…
When did she die?	She died in…

3.4 VOCABULARY FILE
Vocabulary review

1 Match each of the verbs in A with one or more of the nouns in B.

A	B
attend book celebrate do rent stay at take visit	an anniversary a car a conference a hotel a museum photos some sightseeing a table

2 Did I really do it?

Work in groups. Make a true or false statement about yourself, using the verbs and nouns from 1. Your colleagues can ask a maximum of 10 questions to find out if the statements are true or false.

Example *I attended a conference last month.*

Really? Where was it?
What was it about?
Where did you stay?

3 Complete these sentences. The missing words are all in the puzzle below.

Across

1 When I want to drive fast I drive on the *motorway*.

2 Thousands of .... bought tickets to watch the football match.

3 Which country has the best .... for people who love the sun?

4 The flight was good but there was a short .... We left about 10 minutes late.

5 The hotel is in a very good .... It's in the best part of the city and it's very central.

6 There is a high-speed rail .... between Madrid and Seville.

7 Do you think a city has more .... or disadvantages when it hosts a world event?

8 With the choice of Seville for Expo '92, Spain decided on a major investment .... in Andalucia.

9 1992 was the 500th anniversary of the .... of America.

Down

1 I'm afraid he can't speak to you at the moment. He's in a .... with a customer.

2 How did your .... as a wine journalist begin?

3 Millions of TV .... watched the Barcelona Olympics.

4 The Olympic Games were a great .... for Spain.

5 A lot of the money to pay for the Games came from ....

```
A D W O M A D V U L I N K W
P R O J E C T I F L E W R T
E O N T E C W E N T E A E A
T S M O T O R W A Y C C A X
H U E O I M A E T R S A D P
O C T K N O S R E S O R D A
U C U S G D I S C O V E R Y
G E D E L A Y X C A M E A E
H S P E C T A T O R S R N R
T S A C L I M A T E E R K S
C O S T L O C A T I O N Y A
S A D V A N T A G E S I O W
```

4 There are twelve irregular past tense verbs in the puzzle. What are they?

PHOTOCOPIABLE   **3.4**

Grammar cards

good 4.1	bad 4.1	beautiful 4.1	interesting 4.1
dangerous 4.1	safe 4.1	crowded 4.1	noisy 4.1
easy 4.1	busy 4.1	healthy 4.1	enjoyable 4.1
relaxing 4.1	expensive 4.1	cheap 4.1	popular 4.1
boring 4.1	clean 4.1	dirty 4.1	quiet 4.1

Grammar cards

exciting 4.1	difficult 4.1	polluted 4.1	lively 4.1
attractive 4.1	ugly 4.1	adventurous 4.1	famous 4.1
modern 4.1	impressive 4.1	comfortable 4.1	reliable 4.1
economical 4.1	cities 4.1	sports 4.1	fast 4.1
cars 4.1	buildings 4.1	holidays 4.1	leisure activities 4.1

Euroquiz

INFORMATION SHEET 1   STUDENT A

1   Work with Student B. Ask your partner for the information you need to complete this table. Answer your partner's questions.

	FRANCE	GERMANY	ITALY	SPAIN	UK
Geographical area (sq. km)	552,000		301,225		244,046
Life expectancy (years) men		73		74	
Birth rate (per 1,000 population)			10.0		14.0
Cost of living (New York = 100)		115		112	117
Consumption of alcohol (litres per head, per year)		11.8		10.4	
Cars (per 100 people)	42		46		35

Statistics from *The Economist Pocket World in Figures* 1994 Edition

2   Together, use the information in the table to write four more sentences for this Euroquiz. Give your quiz to Students C and D. When they finish, check their answers.

EUROQUIZ

Circle the answer you think is correct.

1 Spain has a larger geographical area than France. T / F

2 The country with the longest life expectancy for men is Italy/Spain/the UK.

3

4

5

6

INFORMATION SHEET 2   STUDENT B

1   Work with Student A. Answer your partner's questions. Ask your partner for the information you need to complete this table.

	FRANCE	GERMANY	ITALY	SPAIN	UK
Geographical area (sq. km)		357,039		504,782	
Life expectancy (years) men	73		73		73
Birth rate (per 1,000 population)	13.3	11.7		11.4	
Cost of living (New York = 100)	137		109		
Consumption of alcohol (litres per head, per year)	12.4		8.9		7.2
Cars (per 100 people)		49		32	

Statistics from *The Economist Pocket World in Figures* 1994 Edition

2   Together, use the information in the table to write four more sentences for this Euroquiz. Give your quiz to Students C and D. When they finish, check their answers.

EUROQUIZ

Circle the answer you think is correct.

1 Spain has a larger geographical area than France. T / F

2 The country with the longest life expectancy for men is Italy/Spain/the UK.

3

4

5

6

4.2 GRAMMAR FILE
Euroquiz

INFORMATION SHEET 3   STUDENT C

1 Work with Student D. Ask your partner for the information you need to complete this table. Answer your partner's questions.

	FRANCE	GERMANY	ITALY	SPAIN	UK
Population (in millions)	56.7			39.1	57.5
Life expectancy (years) women			80		79
Divorce rate (per 1,000 population)		2.0		0.6	
Revenue from tourism ($ million)	21.93		19.7		12.58
Cars (per km of road network)		63		46	
Videos (% of households)	47			43	68

Statistics from *The Economist Pocket World in Figures* 1994 Edition

2 Together, use the information in the table to write four more sentences for this Euroquiz. Give your quiz to Students A and B. When they finish, check their answers.

EUROQUIZ

Circle the answer you think is correct.

1 The roads in Germany are more crowded than in Italy. T / F

2 British/French/Spanish/ women have the longest life expectancy.

3

4

5

6

INFORMATION SHEET 4   STUDENT D

1 Work with Student C. Answer your partner's questions. Ask your partner for the information you need to complete this table.

	FRANCE	GERMANY	ITALY	SPAIN	UK
Population (in millions)		79.6	57.7		
Life expectancy (years) women	81	79		80	
Divorce rate (per 1,000 population)	1.9		0.4		2.9
Revenue from tourism ($ million)		10.94		19.0	
Cars (per km of road network)	35		98		63
Videos (% of households)		51	34		

Statistics from *The Economist Pocket World in Figures* 1994 Edition

2 Together, use the information in the table to write four more sentences for this Euroquiz. Give your quiz to Students A and B. When they finish, check their answers.

EUROQUIZ

Circle the answer you think is correct.

1 The roads in Germany are more crowded than in Italy. T / F

2 British/French/Spanish women have the longest life expectancy.

3

4

5

© Oxford University Press   **PHOTOCOPIABLE**   page 107   **4.2**

Welcome to the York Hotel

❶ Read the hotel information. Then answer the questions below. Use your dictionary to check the meaning of new words.

York Hotel   *Information for guests*

Check-out time — Our normal check-out time is 12 noon. If you wish to leave at a later time, please contact reception.

Early morning calls — To book your early morning call, please dial 24.

Hospitality tray — Complimentary tea- and coffee-making facilities are available. For further supplies, please dial 28.

Room Service — Available 24 hours. Please dial 251 between 7.00 a.m. and 11.00 p.m. and 399 between 11.00 p.m. and 7.00 a.m.

Sandwiches

Cheese	£3.00
Egg Mayonnaise	£2.50
Ham	£3.50
Chicken	£3.50
Soup of the day	£4.00
Fruit in season	£3.00

Dry cleaning and laundry — Available between 7.00 a.m. and 11.00 p.m. Please contact reception.

Fire — For your safety during your stay at the hotel, please read the fire instructions on the back of your hotel door carefully.

Telephone dialling — To call reception, lift the receiver.
To call another room, dial 5, then the number of the room.
To call an outside line, dial 9, then the number you require.
If you have any difficulty, dial 0 for the hotel switchboard.

---

1   What do you do if you want to check out after 12 noon?
2   Which service do you get if you dial 24?
3   Where are the fire instructions?
4   Is there a charge for the tea- and coffee-making facilities in rooms?
5   When are dry cleaning and laundry services available?
6   Can you get room service late at night?
7   How do you get an outside line?
8   Which number do you dial for the hotel switchboard?

❷ Work in pairs. Role-play the telephone conversations between a hotel guest and a hotel employee. Change roles after 3 conversations.

Useful language
Could I (have)…?
I'd like…
Is it possible to (leave)…?

Useful language
Yes, certainly.
Yes, of course.
I'm sorry about that.

Student A
You are a guest at the York Hotel. Phone and ask for the services you need.

1   You have an important meeting tomorrow. You want to wake up at 6.00 a.m.
2   It's 11.30 p.m. and you feel hungry. Order something from Room Service.
3   You would like to make a cup of tea in your room but there isn't any tea left.
4   You would like to leave your suitcase at the hotel for a few hours after you check out.
5   You dialled 9 to get an outside line but didn't succeed.
6   You would like to have decaffeinated instead of caffeinated coffee on your hospitality tray.

Student B
You are an employee of the York Hotel. Answer the phone and respond to the requests from the hotel guest.

Play this game with a partner. Toss a coin. Tails – move one square. Heads – move two squares. Role-play the situations in pairs.

Start

1 You meet a visitor at the airport. Introduce yourself and ask about their flight.

2 Ask a visitor about their home town.

3 Greet a person you know well. Ask about their job or family.

4 A visitor speaks very quickly and you don't understand. What do you say?

5 Phone a company and ask to speak to Marc Brun.

6 Answer the phone for a colleague. Offer to take a message.

7 Introduce a visitor to a colleague.

8 Tell a visitor three things about your home town.

9 Find out what your colleague did last weekend.

10 Your visitor calls you by your family name. Suggest they call you by your first name.

11 You phone a colleague but she's in a meeting. Leave a message.

12 Say goodbye to a visitor at the airport.

13 Telephone the Riviera Hotel and book a room.

14 Check in at the Riviera Hotel. Ask for an early morning call.

15 Check out of the hotel. You want to pay by credit card.

Finish

Grammar cards

Mass 5.1	1 2 3 Count 4 5.1	Mass or Count 1 2 3 4 5.1	some 5.1
some? 5.1	any? 5.1	not ... any 5.1	much? 5.1
not ... much 5.1	many? 5.1	not ... many 5.1	a lot of 5.1
information 5.1	news 5.1	work 5.1	experience 5.1
advice 5.1	equipment 5.1	furniture 5.1	luggage 5.1

Grammar cards

fruit 5.1	machine 5.1	money 5.1	employee 5.1
problem 5.1	wine 5.1	computer 5.1	customer 5.1
book 5.1	time 5.1	exercise 5.1	food 5.1
meeting 5.1	petrol 5.1	cheese 5.1	paper 5.1
water 5.1	letter 5.1	traffic 5.1	alcohol 5.1

5.2 VOCABULARY FILE
I'd like a can of...

1 Write the words from the box in the correct spaces below the pictures.

glass	bottle	packet	carton	bowl	piece	slice	bunch	box	can	tube	jar

a _____ of salami   a _____ of marmalade   a _____ of wine   a _____ of sugar

a _____ of water   a _____ of cake   a _____ of peanuts   a _____ of grapes

a _____ of tomato paste   a _____ of cola   a _____ of matches   a _____ of milk

2 Complete the word lobsters with words from 1 above and from the box below.

bread	biscuits	beer	orange juice	cheese	flowers	jam	salad	toothpaste
honey	meat	cigarettes	chocolates	fruit	rice	strawberries	yoghurt	

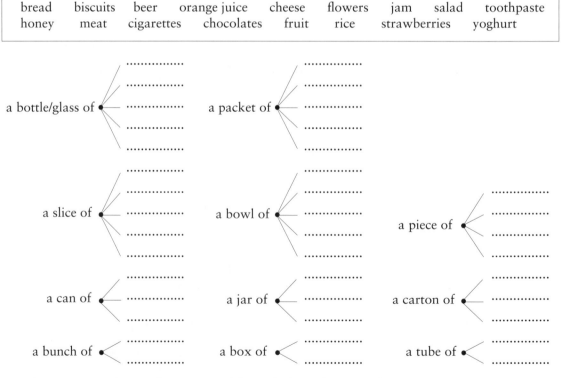

a bottle/glass of
....
....
....
....

a packet of
....
....
....
....

a slice of
....
....
....
....

a bowl of
....
....
....
....

a piece of
....
....
....

a can of
....
....

a jar of
....
....

a carton of
....
....

a bunch of
....
....

a box of
....
....

a tube of
....
....

3 Work in pairs. Student A choose a word from the lists above. Student B make a sentence using the word. Then change.

Example   **Student A**   *cigarettes*
                Student B   *I'd like a packet of cigarettes, please.*

© Oxford University Press

Health and fitness

INFORMATION SHEET 1   STUDENT A

1 Work with Student B. Discuss these questions.

1 Is it important for employers to take an interest in the health of their employees?
2 What sports and fitness facilities should a small company provide? What sports and fitness facilities should a large company provide?
   A gym? A swimming-pool? Keep-fit sessions? Membership at a local sports centre? Other things?

Compare your ideas with the rest of your group.

2 You and your partner have different information from a survey carried out by the magazine *Eurobusiness*.

1 Read the following extract.

FIT AND PROPER

We carried out a survey of the health and fitness facilities provided by 50 top European companies. It was interesting to find how important employee health is in large companies. Some companies subsidize local sports facilities. Other companies keep their employees healthy enough to do a good day's work by fitness training, or a healthy canteen diet.

Company (employees)	Company facilities	In-house food
Carrefour (85,200)	No sports centre.	Wide choice of healthy food available in the canteen.
Repsol (19,600)	Annual bowling championship in which many employees take part.	'Spaniards and health food do not mix.'
Roche (56,600)	Sports centre, swimming-pool, tennis court.	Cards in canteen explain what meals contain and the number of calories.
J Sainsbury (120,100)	Full-time staff run sports facilities with a fitness manager & physiotherapist. Employees encouraged to cycle to work, showers provided on arrival.	Salad bar and vegetarian bar in canteen. Shop sells low-calorie sandwiches.
Siemens (395,000)	Fitness clubs. Lectures on health given to employees.	Organic and vegetarian food available in staff restaurant.

---

2 Exchange information with Student B. Find out:
   which companies provide vegetarian food.
   what kind of gym Cable & Wireless has.
   which company organizes activity clubs.
   which company has no facilities or restaurant for staff.
   what kind of weekend trips Helvetia provides.

3 Which of the following statements do you and your partner agree with?

- A healthy diet is essential for an employee to do a good day's work.
- In-house facilities are better for employees than discount prices at local sports clubs.
- Team sports develop co-operation between employees.
- A healthy staff makes a successful company.

Compare your ideas with the rest of the group.

5.3 SKILLS FILE

Health and fitness

INFORMATION SHEET 2   STUDENT B

1 Work with Student A. Discuss these questions.

1 Is it important for employers to take an interest in the health of their employees?
2 What sports and fitness facilities should a small company provide? What sports and fitness facilities should a large company provide?
   A gym? A swimming-pool? Keep-fit sessions? Membership at a local sports centre? Other things?

Compare your ideas with the rest of your group.

2 You and your partner have different information from a survey carried out by the magazine *Eurobusiness*.

1 Read the following extract.

FIT AND PROPER

We carried out a survey of the health and fitness facilities provided by 50 top European companies. It was interesting to find how important employee health is in large companies. Some companies subsidize local sports facilities. Other companies keep their employees healthy enough to do a good day's work by fitness training, or a healthy canteen diet.

Company (employees)	Company facilities	In-house food
Barclays Bank (98,000)	Small gymnasium (at HQ).	Healthy meals available in staff canteen.
British Airways (49,600)	Gyms, 55 activity clubs, including wine tasting.	Full salad bar, vegetarian choice in canteen.
BTR (130,100)	No sports facilities available.	No staff restaurant.
Cable & Wireless (39,800)	State-of-the-art gym with everything from aerobics to MTV (a satellite TV channel).	Salads and vegetarian meals on offer.
Grand Metropolitan (87,000)	Subsidized membership of local clubs.	Salad bar in the canteen provides healthy option.
Helvetia (4,000)	Weekend skiing trips for employees at subsidized prices.	

---

2 Exchange information with Student A. Find out:
   which company employs a full-time fitness manager and physiotherapist.
   which company has organic food.
   what information the cards in the Roche canteen give.
   what Repsol says about its employees and health food.
   why Sainsbury's provides showers for its employees.

3 Which of the following statements do you and your partner agree with?

- A healthy diet is essential for an employee to do a good day's work.
- In-house facilities are better for employees than discount prices at local sports clubs.
- Team sports develop co-operation between employees.
- A healthy staff makes a successful company.

Compare your ideas with the rest of the group.

6.1 GRAMMAR FILE
What's the mistake?

❶ Each of these sentences has a grammar mistake. Find the mistake, then write the correct sentence.

1 I have flown to the USA three weeks ago.

....

2 In your life, how many different countries did you live in?

....

3 In his present job, he travelled to Europe every month.

....

4 When have you seen her the last time?

....

5 He's not here. He's been to Mexico.

....

6 I've been to Tokyo twice last month.

....

7 She did a lot of work in the last few days.

....

8 I've bought a new car last week.

....

9 How many hours did you work so far this week?

....

10 How long ago have you been to university?

....

❷ Look at your Pocket Book p. 26. Are the sentences below American English or British English? Write the other version.

	American	British	
1 I just had an interview.	❑	❑	....
2 Have you phoned the bank yet?	❑	❑	....
3 They already saw the film.	❑	❑	....
4 I didn't receive your letter yet.	❑	❑	....

What's the value of housework?

INFORMATION SHEET 1   STUDENT A

One of Britain's biggest insurance companies carried out research to find out the value of a housewife's work in the home.

1 Read the results on this sheet, then exchange information with Student B in order to complete the results. Use a dictionary for new words, if necessary.

What's the value of housework?

The Research

The survey covered 1,001 married women with dependent children. The sample was representative of the national population in terms of social class and region. 47% of the sample were housewives, 35% worked part-time and 18% worked full-time.

How many hours do women work?

The research found that housewives spend an average of .... hours a week on domestic work. A woman with a part-time job works an average of .... hours a week at home, while a woman with a full-time job works an average .... hours a week in the home, more than she does in her official job. Hours of work at home decrease sharply as the children get older.

Table 1 shows hours worked by women who have children in each age group:

Age of Children	Hours worked per week
Under 1	.... hrs
Aged 1–4	80 hrs
Aged 5–10	.... hrs
Aged 11–15	.... hrs
Aged 16–17	35 hrs

Table 3 uses the same techniques as Table 2 to put a value on the work of women in paid employment and women with young children.

	£ PER WK	£ PER YR
With a part-time job	293	5,236
With a full-time job	242	12,584
With a child under 1	....	....

What's the value of domestic work?

Table 2 analyses the housewife's average weekly timetable, using wage rates from employment agencies across the country.

Work as a...	Hours worked	£ per hour	£ per week
Nanny	.... hrs	£...........	£...........
Cook	12.2 hrs	£5.35	£65.27
Cleaner	.... hrs	£...........	£...........
Shopper	6.4 hrs	£3.80	£24.32
Dishwasher	5.7 hrs	£3.80	£21.66
Driver	.... hrs	£...........	£...........
Gardener	.... hrs	£...........	£...........
Other	12.3 hrs	£3.60–£4.00	£46.66
Total	**70.7 hrs**		**£348.75**

Comparisons

At £349 a week, or £18,148 a year, a housewife would earn more than 70% of the working population, and more than the average man, who earns £340 a week. The job would also pay more than the occupations in **Table 4**.

	£ PER WEEK
Train driver	£339
Fireman	£...........
Nurse	£320
Social worker	£...........

At £457 a week, a housewife with a child under the age of one would earn more than 85% of the adult population. The job would pay more than the professional and managerial occupations in **Table 5**.

	£ PER WEEK
Production manager	£454
Chemist	£...........
Civil engineer	£451
Teacher	£...........

Source: Legal and General's *Value of a Wife* report

---

2 Work in groups. Discuss these points.

- Did any of the research results surprise you? If so, which ones? Why?
- In your country, do men usually help with the housework?
- Are you in favour of a state salary for housewives with children? Why? Why not?

© Oxford University Press

What's the value of housework?

INFORMATION SHEET 2   STUDENT B

One of Britain's biggest insurance companies carried out research to find out the value of a housewife's work in the home.

1 Read the results on this sheet, then exchange information with Student A in order to complete the results. Use a dictionary for new words, if necessary.

What's the value of housework?

The Research

The survey covered .... married women with dependent children. The sample was representative of the national population in terms of social class and region. .... of the sample were housewives, ... worked part-time and .... worked full-time.

How many hours do women work?

The research found that housewives spend an average of 71 hours a week on domestic work. A woman with a part-time job works an average of 59 hours a week at home, while a woman with a full-time job works an average 49 hours a week in the home, more than she does in her official job. Hours of work at home decrease sharply as the children get older.

Table 1 shows hours worked by women who have children in each age group:

AGE OF CHILDREN	HOURS WORKED PER WEEK
Under 1	90 hrs
Aged 1–4	.... hrs
Aged 5–10	66 hrs
Aged 11–15	55 hrs
Aged 16–17	.... hrs

Table 3 uses the same techniques as Table 2 to put a value on the work of women in paid employment and women with young children.

	£ PER WK	£ PER YR
With a part-time job	....	....
With a full-time job	242	12,584
With a child under 1	457	23,764.

What's the value of domestic work?

Table 2 analyses the housewife's average weekly timetable, using wage rates from employment agencies across the country.

WORK AS A...	HOURS WORKED	£ PER HOUR	£ PER WEEK
Nanny	17.9. hrs	£5.90	£105.61
Cook	.... hrs	£...........	£...........
Cleaner	12.2 hrs	£5.35	£65.27
Shopper	.... hrs	£...........	£...........
Dishwasher	.... hrs	£...........	£...........
Driver	2.6 hrs	£4.50	£11.70
Gardener	1.4 hrs	£5.90	£8.26
Other	12.3 hrs	£3.60–£4.00	£46.66
Total	.... **hrs**		£...........

Comparisons

At £349 a week, or £18,148 a year, a housewife would earn more than 70% of the working population, and more than the average man, who earns £340 a week. The job would also pay more than the occupations in **Table 4**.

	£ PER WEEK
Train driver	£...........
Fireman	£322
Nurse	£...........
Social worker	£331

At £457 a week, a housewife with a child under the age of one would earn more than 85% of the adult population. The job would pay more than the professional and managerial occupations in **Table 5**.

	£ PER WEEK
Production manager	£...........
Chemist	£447
Civil engineer	£...........
Teacher	£436

Source: Legal and General's Value of a Wife report

---

2 Work in groups. Discuss these points.

- Did any of the research results surprise you? If yes, which ones? Why?
- In your country, do men usually help with the housework?
- Are you in favour of a state salary for housewives with children? Why? Why not?

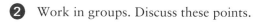

6.3 SKILLS FILE

The interview game

What did you do in your last job? 6.3	What do you do in your present job? 6.3	Do you enjoy travel? 6.3	What do you do in your leisure time? 6.3
Why did you leave your last job? 6.3	Have you done this kind of work before? 6.3	Why do you want to leave your present job? 6.3	Why do you want to work for Summit International? 6.3
What do you think are your strong points? 6.3	What are your ambitions for the future? 6.3	Have you ever had a position of responsibility? 6.3	What salary do you expect? 6.3
When can you start this job? 6.3	Have you had any training since you left school/university? 6.3	Have you ever done any voluntary work? 6.3	Have you discussed this job with your husband/wife/partner? 6.3
What was your favourite subject at school? 6.3	What subject at school did you like least? 6.3	Describe your skills. 6.3	Describe your work experience. 6.3
Have you ever worked in another country? 6.3	Do you speak any foreign languages? 6.3	Ask your own question. 6.3	Ask your own question. 6.3

Board Game

START

FINISH
CONGRATULATIONS! YOU HAVE GOT THE JOB.

INFORMATION OFFICER
Summit International, a leading company in the travel business, is looking for an Information Officer to work on its new travel programmes. The post is a new one, and we require someone with energy and imagination.
GOOD LUCK IN YOUR INTERVIEW.

YOU ARRIVE EARLY. MOVE ON TWO PLACES.

YOU ARE NOT NERVOUS BECAUSE YOU ARE BREATHING DEEPLY. MOVE ON ONE PLACE.

YOU FEEL NERVOUS AND LOSE YOUR VOICE. MISS A TURN.

YOU ARRIVE LATE. GO BACK TWO PLACES.

YOU FORGET TO SHAKE HANDS WHEN YOU LEAVE. MISS A TURN.

YOU IMPRESS THE INTERVIEWER WITH YOUR REPLY. MOVE ON ONE PLACE.

YOU DON'T TELL THE TRUTH ABOUT YOUR WORK EXPERIENCE. MISS A TURN.

YOU ARE FEELING CONFIDENT AND RELAXED. MOVE ON ONE PLACE.

Interviews (1)

❶   Read this description of an interview. You are the candidate. As you read each paragraph, write notes on how you feel at that stage of the interview.

Arriving...

You arrive at the company for the interview. The receptionist doesn't know anything about you. She contacts the personnel department. They are expecting you. The receptionist gives you directions to the fifth floor...

and waiting...

On the fifth floor a secretary says the interviews are running late. You wait for half an hour. Then a door opens and the secretary asks you to come in...

The interview begins...

The interviewer is sitting behind a big desk, reading. You sit on a low, uncomfortable chair, in front of his desk. The interviewer says, 'Good morning', and then continues to read your CV. Suddenly he asks you a lot of questions. Then his phone rings and he answers it...

and continues...

He asks you more questions. Sometimes you don't understand his questions. He often looks at his watch. He takes a lot of notes, too. The answers to some of his questions are in your letter of application. Perhaps he hasn't read it...

and ends...

Suddenly he says 'Right, that's all. Thank you for coming. We'll contact you soon.' You say goodbye and leave. You're still holding your checklist of questions which you didn't ask...

---

❷   Work in small groups.

1   Look at the notes you made while reading. Explain how you felt and why you felt that way. Compare the similarities and differences in your group.

2   Write a checklist of guidelines: *How to give a good interview* or *How to be a good interviewer.* Compare your checklist with other groups.

Interviews (2)

Read these guidelines about giving an interview. Compare it with the checklist you made in Interviews (1).

Preparing for the interview

1 Before the interview, make a checklist of questions to ask the candidate, or of information you need that is not in the CV or letter of application.

2 Arrange the interview room so that you and the interviewee can both sit comfortably and talk face to face. Don't sit behind a desk, or on a chair higher than the candidate's chair. Try to make the interview room as pleasant and welcoming as possible, and put a clock where you can see it during the interview.

3 Make sure the telephone or other people do not disturb you during the interview.

4 Try to make sure that the person who the candidate meets first knows in advance about the interviews, and is polite, friendly, and helpful.

5 Arrange for someone to collect the candidate from Reception.

6 If it's necessary for the candidate to wait, apologize. Offer something to drink.

7 Put some brochures about the company and its products or services for the candidate to read while waiting.

Conducting the interview

1 Give the candidate a friendly welcome and shake hands.

2 Spend time at the beginning making the candidate feel more relaxed.

3 During the interview, ask questions that allow the candidate to talk freely, and avoid Yes/No questions.

4 Try to take notes after the interview, and not during it. If you need to write during the interview, ask the candidate if he/she minds.

5 Body language is important. The expression on your face can encourage or discourage the candidate.

6 Don't ask personal questions too soon. Wait until you have established a rapport.

7 Invite the candidate to ask you questions.

8 Before ending the interview, check your checklist!

9 Tell the candidate when he/she can expect to hear from you. Be as honest as possible about his/her chances.

Vocabulary review

1 Read the clues, and fill in the spaces. All the words are in Unit 6.

#	
1	C
2	A
3	R
4	E
5	E
6	R
7	P
8	R
9	O
10	S
11	P
12	E
13	C
14	T
15	S –

1 a person who gives advice
2 a person who applies for a job
3 a small book which gives you information
4 a person who is receiving training
5 a period of ten years
6 the adjective of *corporation*
7 the noun of apply (not a person)
8 with a lot of energy
9 in all the world
10 holidays on a ship
11 the knowledge or skill you get from doing something, the things that you have done
12 a person who attends an interview
13 imaginative, and with an ability to make new things
14 a list of all the things you can buy from a company
15 a list of the best people for a job

2 Work in groups. Make a chain story.

Student A Make the first sentence of a story with one of the words from the puzzle.
Student B Make the next sentence of the story, using another word.
Student C Make the next sentence, etc.
See how many words you can use. Compare your story with the other groups.

Grammar cards

Past events		Past–present situations

	He bought his car this time last year. 7.1	She qualified as a doctor in 1992. 7.1
She started her present job six months ago. 7.1	They got married in 1990. 7.1	I've known Anton for three years. 7.1
He's owned his car for a year. 7.1	She's been a doctor since 1992. 7.1	I've had my computer for two years. 7.1
They've been married since 1990. 7.1	She's had her present job for six months. 7.1	Pete started work as a teacher in January last year. 7.1

Grammar cards

I met Anton three years ago. 7.1	I bought my computer two years ago. 7.1	He's been a teacher for over a year. 7.1
I got this Walkman a long time ago. 7.1	I've had this Walkman for ages. 7.1	We moved to our flat last month. 7.1
We've been in our flat since last month. 7.1	He became a translator when he left university. 7.1	He's been a translator since he left university. 7.1

GRAMMAR FILE
What's the mistake?

Each of these sentences has a grammar mistake. Find the mistake, then write the correct sentence.

1 I've had my car since a long time.

   ....

2 How long are you working for your company?

   ....

3 I know your sister for a long time.

   ....

4 How many cigarettes have you been smoking this morning?

   ....

5 I am living here since 1992.

   ....

6 How long has she been having her job?

   ....

7 How many years are you teaching English?

   ....

8 How long are they members of the golf club?

   ....

9 He's worked for the same company since ages.

   ....

10 Our business is doing very well since last year.

   ....

P H O T O C O P I A B L E

In-company language training

The large multinational company that you work in wants to improve the English language skills of all its employees. The Training Department has suggested a number of projects but has only enough money to finance two of them this year. You are on the committee which must decide which of the projects below to support.

1   General English classes once a week in-company, and open to all staff.

2   A self-access study room containing a variety of coursebooks, tapes, videos, and a small library.

3   A monthly English language in-house magazine to encourage all staff to read and write articles in English.

4   Study periods abroad to English-speaking countries for selected staff.

5   Corporate membership of a local British Club which offers a programme of regular meetings in English, films, magazines, etc.

6   Exam preparation classes for staff who are interested in taking internationally-recognized English exams.

1   Work in small groups. Decide which two projects you will support.

2   Write a memo to the Head of the Training Department informing him/her of the committee's decisions. Outline the reasons for your choice.

MEMO

To: Date:

From:

Subject:

Vocabulary review

1 Complete the sentences with vocabulary from the box. All the words are in Unit 7.

celebration	abroad	headhunter	surplus	fortunes	boom
deficit	labour costs	freelance	responsibilities		

1 Do you usually spend your holidays .... or in your own country?

2 Production costs in the Far East are usually lower than in Europe because

.... there are often much lower.

3 He works as a .... journalist. He writes articles for several different newspapers and magazines.

4 Our country exports more than it imports, so we have a trade ....

5 They drank a lot of champagne at the .... of their 25th wedding anniversary.

6 The top designers have been so successful financially that they have made

.... from their fashion businesses.

7 After an interview with a .... , he got an offer of a top job with another company.

8 Many countries in the West have a trade .... with Japan.

9 One of her main job .... as personnel manager is selecting and training employees.

10 During a .... , a country's economy grows and businesses do well.

2 Work in pairs. Write a short report or story, using as many as of the words in the box as you can.

Find someone who...

STUDENT A

	Name
is meeting someone after the class	
is going to visit a friend this week	
is going to buy something at the weekend	
is having a meeting at work tomorrow	
is having a business lunch next week	
is going to change his/her job soon	
is going on holiday in the next few weeks	
is taking the train or bus home after class	

Add two questions of your own.

8.1 # Find someone who...

STUDENT B

	Name
is going to start a new hobby soon	
is going shopping tomorrow	
is cooking a meal this evening	
is eating in a restaurant tomorrow	
is travelling on business in the next two months	
is going to take a training course soon	
is going to play a sport at the weekend	
is taking a winter holiday next year	

Add two questions of your own.

© Oxford University Press

The Pacific Hotel in-house newsletter

1 Work in small groups. You are responsible for the first edition of the Pacific Hotel staff newsletter.

Choose a suitable name for the newsletter. Look at the list of items below, and decide who in your group will be responsible for them.

1 You want to include an item on the new manager. These are notes you made at a short interview with him.

> Name: Oliver Thompson. Born U.S.A. Educated Oxford University, and London School of Economics, age 43. Married – 2 children, French wife.
>
> Previous employment: Asst. Manager, Blue Valley International Conference Centre (3 years), Best Eastern Hotels Corporation (Marketing Dept., 10 years).
>
> 'This is going to be the best business hotel in the area...'
>
> 'I am determined to make client comfort a priority...'

Write a short article.

2 The training department wants you to include an announcement about staff training courses in foreign languages. Decide what courses to offer (in-house? abroad? which languages?), how to apply, etc.

Write the announcement.

3 A group of employees wants to organize sports activities for other employees. You received this note from one of them.

> Could you put something in about sports? We want to organize groups for team sports – basketball, football, etc., and competitions for things like swimming, tennis, squash. We'll need to know if people are interested, and arrange a first meeting. Could you write an advertisement for us? They can contact Petra (ext. 2232) for more information – first meeting some time next week? You can suggest the time you think is best. Many thanks.

Write the announcement.

4 Include a short report on the opening ceremony. Here are some notes.

> Champagne reception – well-attended. Goodwill message from the President.
>
> Excellent oriental cuisine, beautiful presentation – well-done the catering team!
>
> Fabulous firework display – music – lights.
>
> A real success!

Write the report.

5 Include at least one other item of your choice – an interview, a feature article, advertisements, etc.

2 When you finish your newsletter, compare it with the other groups.

8.3 SKILLS FILE

Air travel

STUDENT A

You and your partner have information for passengers arriving at either Heathrow or Gatwick airports in London.

1 Read the information for passengers arriving at London Heathrow Airport.
2 Look at Worksheet 1. Prepare the questions you need to ask your partner to complete it.
3 Answer your partner's questions.
4 Ask your partner questions and complete Worksheet 1.

INFORMATION for passengers arriving at London Heathrow Airport

A HOW TO GET INTO CENTRAL LONDON FROM HEATHROW AIRPORT

Distance
Heathrow Airport is approximately 15 miles west of central London.

Transport

Taxi Fare: approximately £34.50.
Journey time: approximately 40 minutes.

Bus Airbus operates to the centre of London, departing every 20 minutes in summer, and every 30 minutes in winter.
Fare: approximately £5.00.
Journey time: approximately 75 minutes, depending on traffic.

Underground The Piccadilly Line serves Heathrow Terminals. Trains depart about every five minutes.
Fare: approximately £2.80.
Journey time: approximately 55 minutes.

B TRANSFERRING FLIGHTS AT HEATHROW

If you checked in your baggage to your final destination, follow the yellow 'Transfers' sign to the Transfer Desk for check-in information. If you checked in your baggage to London only, follow the 'Arrivals' sign and claim your baggage before checking in for your connecting flight.

C TRANSFERRING BETWEEN HEATHROW AND GATWICK

Distance
Heathrow and Gatwick are about 25 miles apart.
Transport
Speedlink coach Departs frequently during the day.
Fare: approximately £13.50.
Journey time: approximately 60 minutes.
Speedlink coaches operate between 0600 and 2200.
747 Jetlink Coach Departs every 30 minutes.
Fare: approximately £9.50.
Journey time: approximately 60 minutes.
747 Jetlink coaches operate between 0500 and 2330.

WORKSHEET 1

INFORMATION for passengers arriving at London Gatwick Airport

A HOW TO GET INTO CENTRAL LONDON FROM GATWICK AIRPORT

Distance to central London ....

Transport	Fare (approx.)	Journey time (approx.)	Frequency
Taxi	£45	....	available 24 hrs
Bus	....	....	....
Train	....	30 mins	....

B CUSTOMS PROCEDURES AT HEATHROW AND GATWICK

Use the BLUE EXIT if: *you started your journey in an EC country*

Use the RED EXIT if: ....

Use the GREEN EXIT if: ....

C BRITISH AIRWAYS LONDON TERMINAL

Location ....

Check-in facilities for British Airways passengers
departing from Gatwick: *full facilities*

departing from Heathrow: ....

Opening hours ....

Check-in time

for international flights: ....

for European services: ....

Air travel

STUDENT B

You and your partner have information for passengers arriving at either Heathrow or Gatwick airports in London.

1 Read the information for passengers arriving at London Gatwick Airport.
2 Look at Worksheet 2. Prepare the questions you need to ask your partner to complete it.
3 Ask your partner questions and complete Worksheet 2.
4 Answer your partner's questions.

INFORMATION for passengers arriving at London Gatwick Airport

A HOW TO GET INTO CENTRAL LONDON FROM GATWICK AIRPORT

Distance
Gatwick Airport is approximately 28 miles south of central London.
Transport
Taxi Fare: approximately £45.00.
Journey time: approximately 1hr 20 minutes.
Bus Speedlink operates Flightline coaches departing every hour to Victoria Coach station.
Fare: approximately £7.50.
Journey time: approximately 1 hour 20 minutes, depending on traffic.
Train British Rail's Gatwick Express runs non-stop to London Victoria every 15 minutes from 0430 to 2200, and hourly at night.
Fare: approximately £8.60.
Journey time: approximately 30 minutes.

B CUSTOMS PROCEDURES AT HEATHROW AND GATWICK

If you started your journey in a European Community (EC) country, you may use the BLUE EXIT. If you started your journey outside the EC, and you have something to declare, go through the RED EXIT. If you started your journey outside the EC, and you have nothing to declare, go through the GREEN EXIT.

C BRITISH AIRWAYS LONDON TERMINAL

Location Victoria Railway Station.
Check-in facilities There are full check-in facilities for all British Airways flights from Gatwick. There is a check-in facility for Heathrow passengers with hand baggage only.
Opening hours The Terminal is open daily from 0630 to 1830.
Check-in time Minimum check-in time before departure is two hours for international flights and one and a half hours for European services.

WORKSHEET 2

INFORMATION for passengers arriving at London Heathrow Airport

A HOW TO GET INTO CENTRAL LONDON FROM HEATHROW AIRPORT

Distance to central London ....

Transport	Fare (approx.)	Journey time (approx.)	Frequency
Taxi	....	40 minutes	available 24 hrs
Bus	....	....	summer...............
			winter..................
Underground	£2.80	....	every 5 minutes

B TRANSFERRING FLIGHTS AT HEATHROW

Follow the yellow 'Transfers' sign to the Transfer Desk if:
....

Follow the 'Arrivals' sign and claim your baggage if:
....

C TRANSFERRING BETWEEN HEATHROW AND GATWICK

Distance between Heathrow and Gatwick ....

Transport	Fare	Journey time (approx.)	Frequency	Hours of operation (approx)
Speedlink Coach	....	....	....	06.00 to 22.00
747 Jetlink Coach	....	....	....	05.00 to 23.30

PHOTOCOPIABLE

Vocabulary review

1 How many collocations relating to air travel can you make from the words in the circle?
Write them below.

arrivals

attendant   window   locker

seat   check   luggage   instructions

flight   board   hand   claim   belt

safety   card   passport   duty-free   departures

announcement   overhead   landing   trolley

life   control   airport   desk   shop

boarding   security   terminal   allowance

jacket   check-in   aisle

baggage

Air travel
airport terminal
....
....
....
....
....
....
....

2 Work in groups. Take turns to say one of the words in the circle.
Score a point for making a correct collocation. Score another point for using the
collocation in a correct sentence.

Example   **Student A**   *locker*
            Student B   *overhead locker.*
                            Be careful when you put your luggage in the overhead locker.

Play this game with a partner. Toss a coin. Tails – move one square. Heads – move two squares. Role-play the situations in pairs.

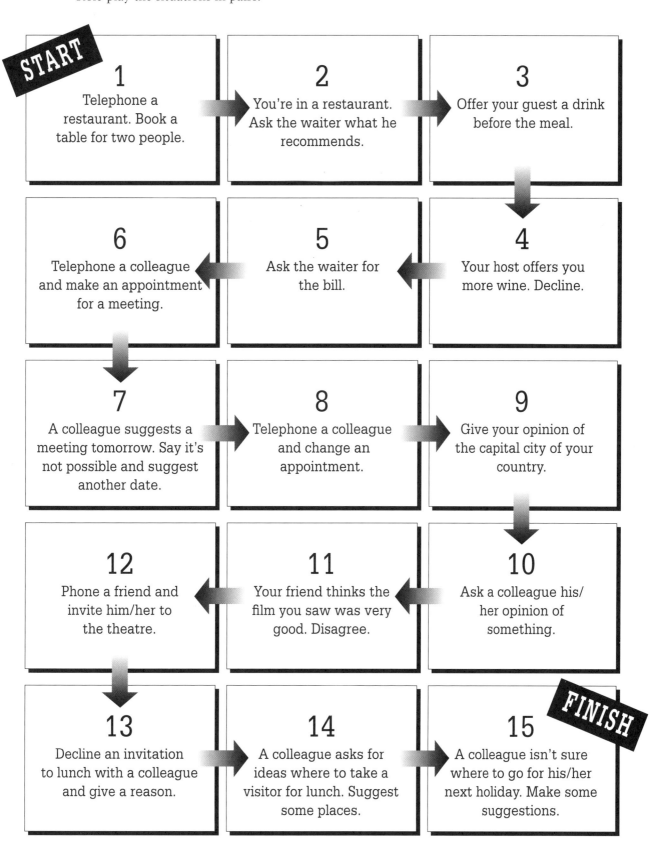

START

1 Telephone a restaurant. Book a table for two people.

2 You're in a restaurant. Ask the waiter what he recommends.

3 Offer your guest a drink before the meal.

6 Telephone a colleague and make an appointment for a meeting.

5 Ask the waiter for the bill.

4 Your host offers you more wine. Decline.

7 A colleague suggests a meeting tomorrow. Say it's not possible and suggest another date.

8 Telephone a colleague and change an appointment.

9 Give your opinion of the capital city of your country.

12 Phone a friend and invite him/her to the theatre.

11 Your friend thinks the film you saw was very good. Disagree.

10 Ask a colleague his/her opinion of something.

13 Decline an invitation to lunch with a colleague and give a reason.

14 A colleague asks for ideas where to take a visitor for lunch. Suggest some places.

15 A colleague isn't sure where to go for his/her next holiday. Make some suggestions.

FINISH

Grammar cards

DEFINITE SITUATIONS/ACTIONS 9.1	**LIKELY SITUATIONS/ACTIONS** 9.1
POSSIBLE SITUATIONS/ACTIONS 9.1	**UNLIKELY SITUATIONS/ACTIONS** 9.1
DEFINITELY NOT SITUATIONS/ACTIONS 9.1	I'm sure … will… 9.1
I think … will… 9.1	Maybe … will… 9.1
I don't think … will… 9.1	I'm sure … won't… 9.1

© Oxford University Press

Grammar cards

Plastic cards will replace cash completely. 9.1	Working hours will get shorter. 9.1
There will be a single currency in Europe. 9.1	There will be more part-time than full-time jobs. 9.1
Manufacturers will make cars of 100% recyclable materials. 9.1	Planes will have a capacity of 800 or more passengers. 9.1
Schoolchildren will learn English from the age of six. 9.1	Many more people will work from home. 9.1
Cigarette smoking will disappear. 9.1	Computers will replace secretaries. 9.1
National boundaries will disappear. 9.1	The problem of global warming will decrease. 9.1

Grammar cards

Future plans, intentions, and decisions *going to* + infinitive 9.2	Fixed future arrangements Present continuous 9.2	Future facts and predictions *will* + infinitive 9.2
Meetings tomorrow? 9.2	A holiday in the summer? 9.2	Next elections in your country? 9.2
Cinema this evening? 9.2	Rate of inflation next year? 9.2	Tomorrow evening? 9.2
Buy a new car in the near future? 9.2	Visitors in the next few days? 9.2	Business trips next week? 9.2
Unemployment decrease in the next few years? 9.2	Changes in your job in the future? 9.2	Sport next weekend? 9.2
English lesson this week? 9.2		

Vocabulary review and extension

1 Match each word in A with a word in B to make a collocation relating to rail travel. Write your answers in the spaces.

A	B	Answers
1 ticket	a. luggage	1 ....
2 waiting	b. train	2 ....
3 buffet	c. board	3 ....
4 left	d. office	4 ....
5 travel	e. car	5 ....
6 commuter	f. room	6 ....
7 season	g. property	7 ....
8 train	h. enquiries	8 ....
9 departures	i. ticket	9 ....
10 lost	j. fare	10 ....

2 Use the words in the box to label the objects in the picture.

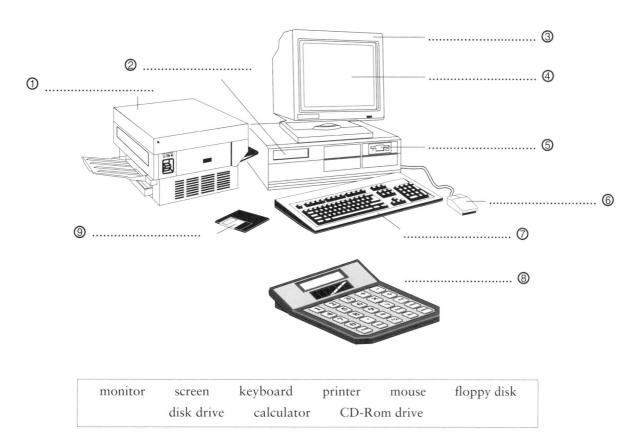

monitor	screen	keyboard	printer	mouse	floppy disk
	disk drive	calculator	CD-Rom drive		

3 Ask the right question

Work in pairs. Choose one of the collocations in **1** or one of the objects in **2**. Ask your partner a question so that he/she will give you the word you chose.

Example   **Student A**   *What can I use to find out 20% of 397?*
           Student B   *A calculator.*

TV across Europe

❶ 1 What kind of programmes do you watch on television? Look at the list below. Add other types of programmes you know.

the news   soap operas   current affairs programmes
films   documentaries   drama series   comedy programmes

2 Discuss these questions.

How many hours television does the average person in your country watch per day, do you think?
What type of programmes are most popular on TV? Why?

❷ Read the text. Fill in the missing information in the chart. What two things do you find most surprising?

What turns viewers on?

The Portuguese watch the most television in Europe, the Swedish view the least, and the highest-rated Greek television show is the midnight news.

These are some of the results from a major European-wide television survey, which the French research group Médiametrie produced. The Eurodata TV report *1993 – One television year in Europe*, discovered trends which were common across Europe. For example, commercial channels are attracting audiences away from public service television.

According to Eurodata, the Portuguese view most television. They watch 258 minutes of television a day – over half-an-hour more than the British, whose daily viewing totals 220 minutes. The Swedes are the least interested in television; they watch for only 125 minutes a day.

There was no link between the number of channels and the time people spend viewing. Most Germans have access to 17 channels, but they spend 80 minutes less a day watching television than the Portuguese, who have only four channels.

The type of programme which attracts audiences is fundamentally different across Europe. The lists of top ten programmes in each country show distinctly national tastes. The list for the Netherlands is all sports programmes, but in Portugal programmes such as soap operas, variety shows, and situation comedies dominate the Top Ten.

Europeans generally like home-grown fiction. It achieves high ratings in most countries. Television producers who hope to enter the European market should concentrate on game shows, according to Eurodata. *Blind Date*, originally an American show, became very successful in Britain, and is also popular in news-hungry Greece.

Adapted from *The European*

Daily TV viewing in minutes		Most watched TV programmes in 1993 in each country	
Portugal	....	Portugal	Pedra Sobre Pedra (soap)
UK	....	UK	Coronation Street (soap)
Italy	210	Italy	Italy/Portugal (soccer)
Spain	200	Spain	Spain/Denmark (soccer)
Ireland	190	Ireland	Eurovision song contest
Greece	185	Greece	News at 24.00 (news)
Germany	....	Germany	Pretty Woman (film)
France	170	France	European Cup final (soccer)
Denmark	140	Denmark	Spain/Denmark (soccer)
Netherlands	139	Netherlands	Poland/Netherlands (soccer)
Northern Belgium	138	Northern Belgium	FC de Kanpisoenen (comedy)
Norway	136	Norway	Dumbo og Maskefjes (detective series)
Sweden	....	Sweden	Kalle Anka och hans vanner (cartoons)

❸ Work in small groups. Choose one of the following activities.
1 You work for a small independent TV company, which wants to sell programmes to countries in Europe. Decide what kind of programme(s) your company will make, and your marketing plan. Present your company plan to the other groups.   *Or*

2 Design one day's television schedule for a new European satellite channel. Present your schedule to the other groups.

Would you...?

❶ Complete the questions, using the correct form of the verbs in brackets.

1 If a friend .... you to his/her wedding next month, what .... you .... ? (invite, wear)

2 If the class .... you to buy a present for your teacher at the end of the course, what .... you .... ? (ask, buy)

3 If you .... enough money to buy any car, which type of car .... you .... ? (have, buy)

4 What .... you .... if someone .... you a scholarship to study any subject? (study, give)

5 What activity .... you .... if you .... on an activity holiday? (choose, go)

6 What .... you .... if somebody .... you a gift voucher to spend on electrical goods? (buy, give)

7 What .... you .... in your suitcase for a holiday in Kenya? (pack)

8 Where .... you .... if somebody .... you a ticket and money to spend for a weekend in any capital city in Europe? (go, offer)

9 If you .... the chance to have dinner with a famous person, who .... you .... ? (have, choose)

10 Where .... you .... for an evening out to celebrate a friend's success? (go)

11 Which language .... you .... if your company .... you a course in another language? (study, offer)

12 What .... you .... if one of your colleagues .... always late? (do, be)

13 How .... you .... the training budget if you .... the personnel officer of your company? (spend, be)

14 What .... you .... if you .... redecorate your office or place of work? (do, can)

15 If you .... your job, what .... you .... ? (change, do)

16 Which month .... you .... if your company .... you to choose any month for your annual holiday? (choose, ask)

17 If your boss .... you a better salary, but you had to move to a smaller town/city, ... you .... ? (offer, accept)

18 If you .... responsible for the entertainment budget in your workplace, what .... you .... the money on? (be, spend)

19 What .... you .... if your boss .... you to do his job while he was on holiday? (say, ask)

20 How .... you .... a presentation in English if your company .... you to represent them at a conference? (prepare, ask)

❷ Choose five questions to ask your colleagues. Carry out a survey. Find out the reasons for their decision. Report back to the class.

Letter writing

1 Dr Janet Jenkins is planning to attend the International Medical Conference in Copenhagen next month. She has written a letter to the organizers, requesting some information.

1 Complete her letter with suitable phrases/words from the boxes below.

Dear Miss Pace

.... (1) regarding the I.M. Conference
in Copenhagen in October, ... (2) if you
would send me the hotel booking details and any other information.
.... (3) that I will speak on 16 October
and .... (4) an outline of my speech, for
you to forward to Mrs H. Ward.
.... (5) let my office know if there are
any problems with the booking arrangements, as I will be out of the country
until 15 October.
.... (6) next month.
Yours sincerely
Janet Jenkins

---

a. further to our telephone conversation	f. I look forward to seeing you
b. could you possibly	g. with reference to
c. I am afraid that	h. request
d. I would be grateful	i. I am pleased to confirm
e. enclose	

2 Write a letter to a colleague working in another country. You recently spoke to him/her on the phone about a professional visit to his/her country/city. You would like some information about the country and some information about hotels. You also want to confirm the exact dates of your visit. Use some of the phrases above.

2 Mr Parker, of CL Computers, is going to visit one of his clients in Rome.

1 Read his letter below. Put it in the correct order.

a. I already have some appointments on 14 and 15 April, and would like to meet you some time on Wednesday 16, perhaps in the morning if that is convenient.
b. Dear Mrs Venitto
c. I hope that we can come to an agreement. I look forward to meeting you next week.
d. I would be very grateful if you could leave a message at my hotel, letting me know what time would suit you.
e. As I mentioned on the telephone last week, I am staying at the International Hotel in Via Romana, between 14 and 17 April. I am arriving on Monday at 12.30 and leaving on Thursday at 9.15.
f. Yours sincerely
g. At that meeting I would like to discuss the percentage discount on large orders, and delivery times.

2 Write a reply. A meeting on 16 April in the morning is not convenient. Suggest a time in the afternoon.

© Oxford University Press

Europe's noisiest country

1   Match the words in the box with their definitions. The first one has been done for you.

| to monitor | a silencer | to install | huge | to make a complaint | a horn |
| chaos | a whistle | to suffer | to estimate | a siren | ~~to long for~~ · |

1   to want something very much *to long for*

2   to calculate the cost or size of something approximately ....

3   to experience something unpleasant or painful ....

4   the opposite of very small ....

5   to say you are not happy with, or dissatisfied about something ....

6   police cars, fire-engines, and ambulances have one of these to warn people ....

7   drivers use this part of a car to make a loud warning sound ....

8   this reduces the noise made by a car or motorbike ....

9   a traffic policemen uses this instrument to attract attention when controlling traffic ....

10   a state of great disorder or confusion ....

11   to put a new piece of equipment or machinery into place, ready for use ....

12   to check, record or test something regularly for a period of time ....

2   Read the article. Note the key points.

SPANIARDS LONG FOR THE SOUND OF SILENCE

Spain is the noisiest country in Europe, according to the Organisation for Economic Co-operation and Development. It estimates that 23% of the population is exposed to noise levels above the World Health Organisation limit of 65 decibels – compared with 8% in Germany, 13% in France and 20% in Greece. Eighty per cent of the noise comes from traffic – the result of the huge increase in the number of cars and the growth of cities. A 1993 survey of Madrid showed that 69% of the population suffered daily noise levels above the 65 decibel limit. Even in August, which is the quietest month because a third of Madrid's population is away on holiday, there were more than 2,000 complaints about noise.

The Madrid study showed that noise caused learning difficulties among children at school. Other studies have shown that noise over long periods causes stress, nervous, and digestive problems.

'There are many causes', says Madrid's mayor. 'Motorbikes, sirens, alarms, televisions, and people singing in the streets make rest impossible.' The noise problem is worst in the narrow streets of Madrid's old town, where horn-happy drivers in traffic jams, 'macho' motorbikes without silencers, and the whistles of traffic policemen trying to control the chaos all increase the volume of noise.

But traffic is not the only cause of the problem. According to one government minister, the 'Mediterranean character' is an important factor. 'To a Mediterranean noise means enjoyment, and the more people enjoy themselves, the more noise they like to make.'

Madrid's response to the problem has been to install a system to monitor noise levels, making it the first city in Europe to do so. The system, costing $700,000, will also measure air pollution, another of the city's big problems. The government has taken the first important step, but it knows that solving the problem will be a lot more difficult than measuring it.

Adapted from *The European*

3   Use your notes to make a brief presentation about noise problems in Spain.

4   Work in groups. Discuss the following questions.
- Which is the noisiest city you have visited?
- Is noise a problem where you live? If so, what problems have you experienced?
- Have you ever made complaints about noise? To whom? What was the result?
- What would you do to reduce the noise in cities? Make a list of key points and present your findings to the class.

Motivating staff

1 Some companies offer their employees fringe benefits, for example, a company car, a subsidized staff restaurant. Read the list below and tick the fringe benefits your company offers. Check new words in a dictionary, if necessary.

COMPANY PERKS

childcare allowance/workplace nursery	subsidized canteen	free tea and coffee
sports and social club	private health insurance	pension scheme
life assurance	mortgage subsidy	luncheon vouchers
expense account	staff discount	profit share
performance bonus	annual bonus	
company car	annual season ticket loan	
relocation expenses	(interest-free)	

---

2 Read these job advertisements and underline the fringe benefits they mention.

TOURISM MARKETING ASSISTANT
London
£14,850-£16,250

The Tourism Department of Easton City Council is responsible for tourism, the arts, and museums. We now have a vacancy for a Tourism Marketing Assistant in our busy friendly office.
You will report to the Tourism Marketing Manager and you will be responsible for preparing leisure publications, organizing exhibitions, and dealing with conference enquiries.
You should have a background in tourism, ideally with an appropriate qualification. A foreign language would be an asset. Initiative, enthusiasm, tact and a sense of humour are also important.
In return we are offering an excellent package which includes 25 days' holiday, luncheon vouchers, health and pension schemes, interest-free season ticket loan, and childcare allowance.

For an application form and further details, call 0181 666 9292 (24 hours) quoting ref: TMA/95.

Computer Officer   **A B I C A R D**

Abicard has an impressive record of growth and profitability. This is due in part to the bank's Information Systems Section. We are developing our sophisticated IT systems further and a person is needed to liaise with users and with other IT staff to provide a comprehensive support service for the network.
We are looking for a computer science graduate with a strong background in systems programming, with specialist expertise in PC systems on a network. We need someone who is adaptable, with the ability to master detail quickly, and capable of working under pressure.
Career prospects are excellent and there is an attractive package which will reflect your qualifications and experience. Benefits include flexible working hours, relocation assistance, mortgage subsidy, pension scheme and life assurance.

Application forms are available from: The Personnel Department, Abicard House, Southampton SO17 2BY.

Compare your answers with your partner.

3 Work in pairs. Make a list of other fringe benefits your company offers, and other fringe benefits you can think of. Compare your list with the rest of the class.

4 Read the information about these two people. What fringe benefits do you think would be most useful for them? Choose from your own ideas and from the list in 1.

Nicola Williams is married with three children (aged 6, 4, and 2). She has a job in Personnel Management at *Baby and Child*, a large, national company which sells clothing and equipment for babies and children. As soon as she got her new job a year ago, her husband was made redundant, so at the moment he stays at home to look after the two younger children. Because there is no suitable public transport she drives the 25 km to work each day.

Steven Barton is 25 years old and is not married. He has worked at *Worldwide Airlines* office in central London for seven years, since he left school. He is buying a flat in a suburb, about an hour by tube from his work. He lives alone and does not spend much time in his flat. His hobbies include all types of sport. He plays different sports at least three times a week, he goes skiing every winter, and he goes on watersports holidays abroad in the summer. While he has been with *Worldwide* he has done a course in Tourism and hopes to study more in the future.

5 Work in groups of 3 or 4. Discuss these questions.
- If you could choose, which fringe benefits would you select? Why?
- Would you rather have a higher salary or more fringe benefits? Why?
Do you all agree?
Compare your answers with the other groups.

Wordbuilding and wordstress

1 We can make nouns from the adjectives and verbs in the box below by adding one of these suffixes:

-ment   -ity   -ness   -tion

Use the words in the box to complete the word lobsters. Be careful. The spelling often changes. Check in your dictionary.

develop	tired	explain	happy	connect	possible	improve	fit
popular	announce	reduce	real	describe	require	sad	reserve
punctual	kind	achieve	secure	active	govern	stiff	cancel

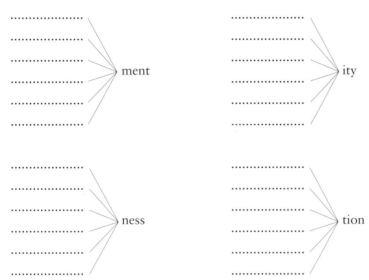

....
....
....
.... ⟩ ment
....
....

....
....
....
.... ⟩ ity
....
....

....
....
.... ⟩ ness
....
....

....
....
....
.... ⟩ tion
....
....

2 Write the nouns from the word lobsters under the correct stress pattern.

● ●   ● ● ●   ●●● ●   ● ●●   ● ● ● ●   ● ●●●●

tiredness   *requirement*   *development*   *happiness*   *explanation*   *possibility*

3 Work in a circle. In turn, each student asks a question using an adjective or verb from the box. The next student answers the question using the noun, then asks another question. A correct answer scores a point.

Example
Student A *Football is a very **popular** sport.*
Student B *Yes, its **popularity** has increased a lot recently.*
Student C *Have you **cancelled** the appointment?*
Student D *No, …*

Or

Work in groups. Make a chain story.
Student A Make the first sentence of a story using one of the words from the box.
Student B Make the next sentence of the story, using another word.
Student C Make the next sentence, etc.
See how many words you can use. Compare your story with the other groups.

Another country

Article 1
Read the article and complete the chart on page 146.

Bullfights in a crossword puzzle

At the age of 19, Michael Robinson became Britain's most expensive teenage footballer when he was transferred to Manchester City for $756,000. In 1987 he went to play for Osasuna in the Spanish First Division. Today he is a football commentator on television. He lives in Madrid with his wife and two children.

What were your first impressions of Spain?
Like most people when they come to Spain, I expected it would be all flamenco, sombreros, and bullfighting. But Pamplona, where I first lived when I joined Osasuna, wasn't like that at all. My first thought was 'Oh, my God, it's all concrete buildings!' But then I discovered Pamplona had an atmosphere that I liked very much.

Was the language a problem to start with?
Yes, it was like a big crossword puzzle. Nobody at the football club spoke English, so I just waltzed around with my verb book and dictionary. I soon realised that it's very important not to take yourself too seriously and to let people laugh at you.

What do you like best about living in Spain?
The passion. People in Spain either really love things or they don't like them at all. When they go out they make sure they enjoy themselves, or they don't go out at all. I enjoy the energy and the passion that surrounds the Spaniards.

Did you see yourself staying this long when you originally came to play for Osasuna?
At first I just thought I'd learn a different side of football and a bit of the language. But then I fell in love with Spain. It wasn't love at first sight, but when I retired from football and went home for a short time, I really missed Spain. I often went to a restaurant which a Spaniard from Ciudad Real owned, just so I could speak to him.

Is there anything you miss about England?
I miss silly things like television, but not much else.

Can you see yourself going back to England permanently?
Yes, I can imagine it, but I don't know when, and I don't know why.

Michael Robinson was talking to Harvey McGavin.

Adapted from *The European*

Article 2
Read the article and complete the chart on page 146.

A Sardinian in the suburbs

Alessandro 'Alex' Mascia, 32, is a chef from Cagliari in Sardinia. In 1979 he left Italy for Paris, where he attended a cookery school. He has been living in England since 1983, and in 1987 he opened a very successful Italian restaurant in a London suburb.

Why did you decide to leave your country at such an early age?
I have always wanted to travel; to get to know new things. I get tired of places and situations very quickly. I went to France to learn about French cooking, but I prefer Italian cooking; it's less complicated, closer to its traditions. Then I realized you really need to be able to speak English to do anything, and I moved to Britain to study and worked in Italian restaurants to support myself.

What do you like most about Britain?
The freedom it gives you to be who you want to be, without worrying what the neighbours will say.

Why did you open a restaurant in an area which is quite poor and not very lively at night?
I did not have a lot of money to begin with; it was all I could afford. I have been very lucky because the message started to travel. People even came from other districts and they returned with their friends.

What do you like about the British people?
The British have surprised me a lot. They are a lot more adventurous than I expected. They are ready to try out all sorts of dishes, and they appreciate quality and variety – that's very important for a chef.

What do you miss most about Italy?
The sun, of course, but also the choice of ingredients and the quality of the food. When I first came to England you could not buy mozzarella cheese in London. Things have changed now and you can find a good choice of Italian cheeses in major supermarkets.

Do you think you will ever go back to Sardinia?
I am extremely tempted. When I return for a holiday it seems like a vision of heaven: it's sunny, there are mountains and sea all around, and you can get delicious fresh fish every day. I ask myself what I am doing in grey, rainy, England. But I know that if I made Sardinia my home again, I'd soon get bored. I was born restless and I hope to die that way.

Alessandro Mascia was talking to Paola Buonadonna.

Adapted from *The European*

Another country

Article 3
Read the article and complete the chart on page 146.

A German who followed her nose

Karoline Vieth is a perfume creator, or *nez*, who moved from her home in Holzminder, Germany, to live in Paris. She develops new aromas for cosmetics and perfumes.

Why did you move to Paris from Germany?
Love… and also work. The company that I work for is German, and I have created perfumes for them in Germany, New York and Tokyo. But Paris is the best place for creating a perfume. All the raw materials usually come from the south of France, so to create perfume in France's most celebrated city makes complete sense.

Is there anything you dislike about living and working in Paris?
The traffic! And sometimes the different attitude to work. Germans are more organized. In Germany, if a meeting is scheduled first thing in the morning, everyone is always there on time. In France nobody would be there. One must be very patient. It tends to be less strict here, and therefore less organized. And Parisians are difficult; they tend to be rude, especially in the stores.

What do you like most about Paris?
There is always something to do in Paris. There are lots of films, plays, clubs and exceptional restaurants in every neighbourhood. I am from Holzminder in Germany, which is a much smaller city than Paris. Since I have been here, I go out ten times more than I did back home.

Has your move to Paris from Germany helped you create perfumes?
Absolutely. Paris is a city that offers you ideas. I find that most of my inspiration comes from looking at the people. It's hard to explain, but Parisian women seem to have more style, they just know how to put everything together and make it look great. German women are not as risky; they are far more conservative.

Which perfume do you wear?
I prefer Paloma Picasso for myself, a French perfume which I did not help to create.

Karoline Vieth was talking to Joanne Bean.

Adapted from *The European*

Article 4
Read the article and complete the chart on page 146.

The Dane who went south

Ole Jorgensen, a Danish jazz drummer, lives with his Italian wife on a farm in Latina, south of Rome. He teaches music and from time to time plays with pianist Enrico Pierannunzi, as well as encouraging other Scandinavians to come to Italy to perform.

Did you find it hard adapting to the Italian way of life?
I found it really difficult to get used to the confusion and lack of organization in Italy. Italy has the same geographical problems of a country like Chile because of the distance from north to south. The way of thinking changes a lot as you move south.

What's the biggest difference from Denmark you've noticed?
During the 20 years I've been in Italy I've frequently experienced the problem of people not working together. Denmark is different. We are like a football team which plays together to get a result. In Italy, everyone plays on their own.

What do you like most about Italy?
I love the climate, and the chance to eat all that fresh produce, like olives and grapes. I really miss them when I'm back in Denmark.

Which is your favourite Italian city?
Any of the cities of art, but especially Rome. But it's difficult to live here because of the pollution.

Have you any observations about Italy's young generation?
The majority continue to live with their family even when they are adults. In Denmark young people receive government help when they are studying. In Italy they have to depend on their families.

Do you think you will leave Italy soon?
No. When I return to Denmark, I always miss the Italian way of life.

Ole Jorgensen was talking to Rossella Lorenzi.

Adapted from *The European*

11.2 SKILLS FILE
Another country

1 Complete the chart with information from the articles.

Name	**Article 1** Michael Robinson	**Article 2** Alex Mascia	**Article 3** Karoline Vieth	**Article 4** Ole Jorgensen
Moved from	....	....	....	....
Lives in	....	....	....	....
Reason for moving to another country	....	....	....	▬▬▬
	....	....	....	▬▬▬
	....	....	....	▬▬▬
	....	....	....	▬▬▬
Problems/difficulties	....	....	....	....
	....	....	....	....
	....	....	....	....
Likes	....	....	....	....
	....	....	....	....
	....	....	....	....
Dislikes	▬▬▬	....	....	....
	▬▬▬	....	....	....
Things missed	....	....	▬▬▬	▬▬▬
	....	....	▬▬▬	▬▬▬
Does he/she want to return to his/her own country?	....	....	▬▬▬	....

2 Work in pairs. Discuss the following questions.
- Which two things do you find interesting or surprising? Why?
- Imagine you live in another country. What would you miss?

Social responses

Thank you so much for your help. 11.3	Sorry, I've spilt some coffee on the table. 11.3	I'm sorry I'm late. 11.3	Do you mind if I smoke? 11.3
Do you mind if I open the window? 11.3	Could I borrow your dictionary? 11.3	Could I use your phone? 11.3	Have a good weekend. 11.3
Would you like another drink? 11.3	I didn't get the job I wanted. 11.3	May I sit here? 11.3	I've won a holiday in California! 11.3
Don't mention it. 11.3	Don't worry. 11.3	It doesn't matter. 11.3	No, not at all. 11.3
Well, I'd rather you didn't. 11.3	Yes, certainly. 11.3	Please do. 11.3	Thanks, and the same to you. 11.3
Thanks, but not at the moment. 11.3	Oh, I'm sorry to hear that. 11.3	Yes, of course. 11.3	Congratulations! 11.3

12.1 GRAMMAR FILE
Describing a process

❶ Read this description. A producer is talking about the production process of *prosciutto crudo*, an Italian dried meat. Number the paragraphs in the correct order.

THE MAKING OF ITALIAN *PROSCIUTTO CRUDO*

☐ a.

We leave the meat in the cool room for ten or twelve months, or longer, until it reaches maturity. By this time it has the taste and bouquet of a good *prosciutto*. Finally we distribute it and sell it to the customer.

☐ b.

The salt draws the water out of the *prosciutto* and it loses weight as a result. Then we wipe the salt off and leave the meat to dry for a few weeks.

☐ c.

After the initial drying process, we wash the meat and spread a mixture of pepper, salt, and fat in order to prevent excessive dehydration. After that we put it in a cool room where we regulate the temperature and the flow of air.

☐ d.

The first thing we do is choose the right meat. We use only the best meat to make *prosciutto crudo*. It comes from a special breed of pigs which we chose because of the quality of their meat.

☐ e.

Then, the first stage in the production process is salting. We spread salt all over the meat by hand. In Italy we use small amounts of salt. That is why Italian *prosciutto* is sweeter than others.

---

❷ Complete these sentences which describe how *prosciutto crudo* is made. Use the information from the paragraphs above.

Example   *Only the best meat is used to make* prosciutto crudo.

1 The meat comes from pigs which .... for the quality of their meat.

2 In the first stage of the production process salt .... all over the meat by hand. In Italy small amounts of salt ....

3 The water .... out of the *prosciutto* by the salt and weight

.... as a result.

4 Then the salt .... off and the meat .... to dry for a few weeks.

5 Next the meat .... and a mixture of pepper, salt and fat

.... all over it, in order to prevent excessive dehydration.

6 After that the meat .... in a cool room where the temperature and the

flow of air ....

7 The meat .... in the cool room for ten or twelve months, or longer, until it reaches maturity and has the taste and bouquet of a good *prosciutto*.

8 Finally it .... and it .... to the customer.

❸ Work in pairs. Think of a process you know well. Describe it. Use these expressions.

In the first stage of the process, ...	Next, ...	Then, ...	After that, ...	Finally, ...

PHOTOCOPIABLE   © Oxford University Press

Safety on the roads

1 Complete this article. Use the correct passive form of the verb in brackets.

Designs on making our roads safer

Would you travel by plane if a total of 50,000 people were killed in plane crashes every year? Probably not. It's difficult to believe it, but that's how many people ....[1](kill) on the European Union's roads every year. That's the same as a jumbo jet crashing every seventeen hours, killing everybody on board. Since the European Community ....[2](found) in the 1950s, over two million people ....[3](kill) in road accidents. In the same period, more than forty million ....[4](injure). That's more than the total population of Spain, or the combined population of Portugal, Belgium, and the Netherlands. But fortunately the news is not all bad and in recent years, big improvements ....[5](make), particularly in Britain and the US.

As a result of stricter safety regulations which ....[6](introduce) in the US at the beginning of the 1990s, the number of road deaths ....[7](reduce) from a peak of 57,000 in 1969 to 39,000 in 1992. In Britain, road casualties in 1992 were the lowest since records ....[8](start) in 1922. That's a significant decrease because road traffic has increased several hundred times during that period.

According to the European Transport Safety Council, car safety standards in Europe are 20 years behind the times. The ETSC wants very strict safety regulations which will force manufacturers to design much safer cars. 'If stricter regulations ....[9](introduce), car producers ....[10](force) to make safety their priority', said a Safety Council spokesman. 'This is the only way that Europe's terrible figure of nearly 1000 road deaths every week ....[11](reduce).'

2 Work in groups. Make a list of measures which could help to reduce road deaths.

Example *lower speed limits*

Which do you think is most important? Which is least important?
Compare your list with other groups.

Play this game with a partner. Toss a coin. Tails – move one square. Heads – move two squares.
Role-play the situations in pairs.

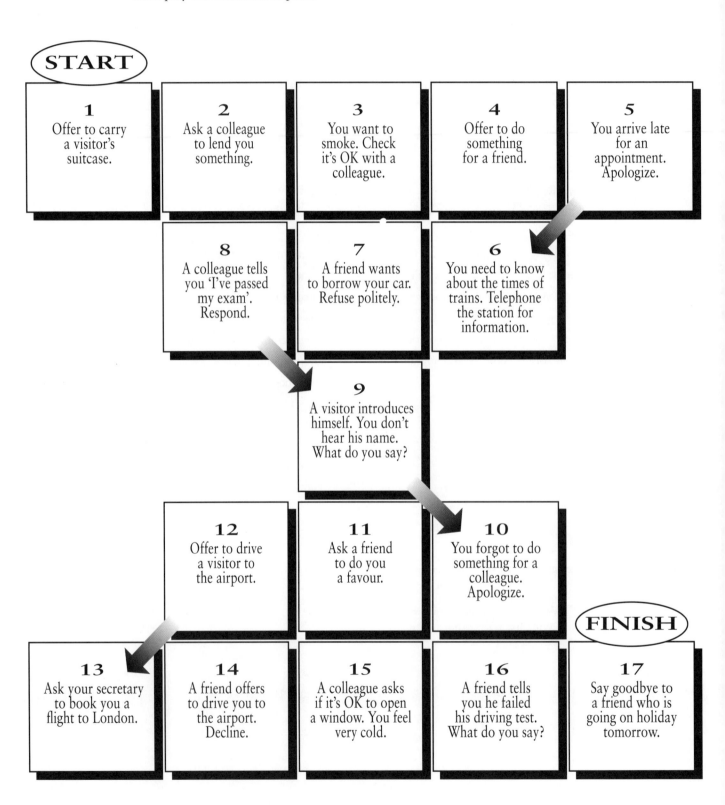

START

1
Offer to carry
a visitor's
suitcase.

2
Ask a colleague
to lend you
something.

3
You want to
smoke. Check
it's OK with a
colleague.

4
Offer to do
something
for a friend.

5
You arrive late
for an
appointment.
Apologize.

8
A colleague tells
you 'I've passed
my exam'.
Respond.

7
A friend wants
to borrow your car.
Refuse politely.

6
You need to know
about the times of
trains. Telephone
the station for
information.

9
A visitor introduces
himself. You don't
hear his name.
What do you say?

12
Offer to drive
a visitor to
the airport.

11
Ask a friend
to do you
a favour.

10
You forgot to do
something for a
colleague.
Apologize.

FINISH

13
Ask your secretary
to book you a
flight to London.

14
A friend offers
to drive you to
the airport.
Decline.

15
A colleague asks
if it's OK to open
a window. You feel
very cold.

16
A friend tells
you he failed
his driving test.
What do you say?

17
Say goodbye to
a friend who is
going on holiday
tomorrow.

Requesting and giving information

INFORMATION SHEET 1 STUDENT A

Useful language	

I saw your advertisement in…
 Could you please send me…
 Please send me further details of…
 I am interested in…
 I would like more
   information about…
	Thank you for your letter/fax.
	 Please find enclosed…
	 If you require any further
	   information, please…
	 Do not hesitate to contact us if…

Task 1

You see this advertisement in a magazine. Choose one of the activities and write/fax for a brochure. You also want to know the dates of these holidays, and what sort of accommodation is available. Give your letter/fax to Student B.

ACTIVITY & LEISURE HOLIDAYS

SCOTLAND

Scotland is the ideal place for a superb range of active holidays including golf, fishing, skiing, sailing, riding, windsurfing, bowling, gliding and much, much, more…

Send for a free colour brochure to:

SCOTHOLS, 64 George St, Edinburgh EH2 2YS

Task 2

You work for Dean Park College and receive a letter/fax from Student B. Use the information below to write a reply.

DEAN PARK COLLEGE

DATES	COURSE	MAXIMUM NUMBERS	OTHER INFORMATION
June 15-29	English + sailing	5	No experience necessary
July 2-16	English + golf	10	Golf handicap necessary
July 17-31	English + fishing	12	Beginners welcome
August 2-16	English + watersports	5	No experience necessary

Requesting and giving information

INFORMATION SHEET 2   STUDENT B

Useful language	
I saw your advertisement in…	
Could you please send me…	Thank you for your letter/fax.
Please send me further details of…	Please find enclosed…
I am interested in…	If you require any further
I would like more	information, please…
information about…	Do not hesitate to contact us if…

Task 1

You see this advertisement in a magazine. Choose one course combination and write/fax for a brochure. You also want to know if you need any particular experience for the activities, and information about the dates of the courses. Give your letter/fax to Student A.

DEAN PARK COLLEGE

LANGUAGE & ACTIVITY COURSES

Improve your English language skills this summer AND play golf, go salmon fishing, or try sailing. Send for a free colour brochure to: Dean Park College, 2 Park Crescent, Edinburgh EH4 1QZ

Task 2

You work for Scothols and receive a letter from Student A. Use the information below to write a reply.

SCOTHOLS

TIME OF YEAR	AREA	ACTIVITY	ACCOMMODATION
Dec–April	Cairngorms	Skiing, snowboarding	Self-catering chalets
March–Oct	Highlands	Fishing	3–4 star hotels
May–Sept	West Coast	Sailing, windsurfing	4–8 berth yacht
March–Oct	Borders	Pony-trekking	Bed & Breakfast (farms)
All year	Various	Golf, bowling, gliding	Hotels and B&B

Making and replying to invitations

INFORMATION SHEET 1   STUDENT A

> **Useful language**
>
> We would like to invite you to…
> We would be very pleased if you could…
>
> I would be delighted to accept your invitation to…
> Unfortunately, I am unable to accept your invitation to…

Task 1

The organization you work for is arranging a Food & Fitness Day for employees. Your boss asked you to invite a well-known food expert, Anton Merrimann, who writes for a newspaper and presents food programmes on TV, to give a talk and short demonstration about food and cooking for professional people with an active lifestyle.

Using the information below, write a letter to invite him. Outline the proposed programme, and check that the morning session is convenient for him.

Give your letter to Student B.

Food & Fitness Day

A one day practical session for <u>all</u> staff on Wednesday, August 8.

10.00 – 12.00	Food and an active lifestyle (talk and demonstration)
12.00 – 14.00	Vegetarian lunch (buffet)
14.00 – 16.00	Physical exercise for professional people (wear loose clothing)
16.00 – 17.00	Questions & Answers (panel discussion)

Task 2

You are Katie Cook, a well-known fitness and health expert. You receive a letter from Student B inviting you to give a talk.

Write a letter to accept the invitation, but say you prefer to talk in the morning.

Making and replying to invitations

INFORMATION SHEET 2   STUDENT B

Useful language
We would like to invite you to...
We would be very pleased if you could...
I would be delighted to accept your invitation to...
Unfortunately, I am unable to accept your invitation to...

Task 1

The organization you work for is arranging a Food & Fitness Day for employees. Your boss asked you to invite a well-known fitness expert, Katie Cook, who presents fitness and workout programmes on TV, to give a talk and short demonstration on fitness and exercise for professional people.

Using the information below, write a letter to invite her. Outline the proposed programme, and check that the afternoon session is convenient for her.

Give your letter to Student A.

Food & Fitness Day

A one day practical session for all staff on Wednesday, August 8.

10.00 – 12.00	Food and an active lifestyle (talk and demonstration)
12.00 – 14.00	Vegetarian lunch (buffet)
14.00 – 16.00	Physical exercise for professional people (wear loose clothing)
16.00 – 17.00	Questions & Answers (panel discussion)

Task 2

You are Anton Merrimann, a well-known food expert. You receive a letter from Student A inviting you to give a talk.

Write a letter declining the invitation, as you have another appointment on the same date. Suggest the name of a colleague who they could invite in your place.

Making and confirming a booking

INFORMATION SHEET 1   STUDENT A

Useful language

We are holding a (conference)...
The (conference) will take place...
We require.../We would like...
Please confirm our booking...
I would like to book accommodation for...
I would like to reserve...

I am writing to confirm...

Task 1

Your company is holding a one-day conference. Your boss has asked you to make a booking at a local hotel. Using the information below, write the booking letter you send.

Hotel venue:	Forum International
Contact:	Wendy Richards, Conference Co-ordinator
Date:	24 September
Number of Delegates:	40
Facilities required:	Meeting room, OHP and flip-chart
Refreshment:	Coffee (10.30) Lunch (12.00–13.00, 3 course) Tea (16.00)

Give your letter to Student B.

Task 2

Two days before the conference, the main speaker, Mr P. Jones, asks you to arrange overnight accommodation for him after the conference. He wants a single room and breakfast. Fax the hotel.

Give your fax to Student B.

Task 3

You work for a hotel, *Astra International*, and receive a letter from Student B. Write to confirm the reservation for the trade fair.

Task 4

You work for a hotel, *Astra International*, and receive a fax from Student B. Reply to the fax. You have only four single rooms available. Suggest a nearby hotel.

Making and confirming a booking

INFORMATION SHEET 2 STUDENT B

Useful language

We are holding a (conference)…
The (conference) will take place…
We require…/We would like…
Please confirm our booking…
I would like to book accommodation for…
I would like to reserve…

I am writing to confirm…

Task 1

Your company is holding a one-day trade fair. Your boss has asked you to make a booking at a local hotel. Use the information below to write the booking letter you send.

Hotel venue:	Astra International
Contact:	Jackie Buckland, Exhibitions Co-ordinator
Date:	31 August
Number of exhibitors:	approx. 25
Facilities required:	Large exhibition area, 6 small meeting rooms
Refreshment:	Coffee & tea all day, buffet lunch (12.00–14.00)

Give your letter to Student A.

Task 2

Two days before the trade fair, six of the exhibitors ask you to arrange overnight accommodation for them after the trade fair. They want single rooms and breakfast. Fax the hotel.

Give your fax to Student A.

Task 3

You work for a hotel, *Forum International*, and receive a letter from Student A. Write and confirm the reservation for the conference.

Task 4

You work for a hotel, *Forum International*, and receive a fax from Student A. Reply to the fax. There are no rooms available. Suggest a nearby hotel.

 © Oxford University Press

Banks

1 Label the pictures with the correct word from the box.

> coins
> (bank)notes
> plastic cards
> traveller's cheques
> eurocheque
> exchange rates
> cash dispenser
> account number

....

....

....

....

....

....

....

....

2 Look at the following methods of payment.

cash   by   cheque   eurocheque   traveller's cheque

(to pay)

by bank transfer   by   credit card   payment card

Think of three things you often buy. How do you pay for them?
Which other methods do you use? When do you use them?

3 Put this conversation between a bank cashier and a customer in order. Number the boxes.

☐ Would you sign each cheque, please?

☐ I'd like to cash some traveller's cheques, please.

☐ Right. That's three ten-pound notes and four fives. Fifty pounds in total.

☐ Certainly. Have you got any identification on you?

☐ Yes, here's my passport.

☐ Thank you. That's fine. How would you like the money?

☐ Fine. Can I borrow your pen?

☐ Three ten, and four five-pound notes, please.

4 Work in pairs. Practise the conversation in 3. Change roles and practise again.

5 Use words from the box to complete the conversation.

| guarantee card   date   amount   to cash   notes   signature   card number |

Customer: I'd like ....¹ a eurocheque, please.

Cashier: Certainly. Could I see your eurocheque ....² please?

Customer: Yes, of course.

Cashier: Thank you. Would you complete the details on the cheque? That's the ....³, the ....⁴, the place, and your ....⁵ And please write your ....⁶ in the space on the back of the cheque.

Customer: Right. Could I have the cash in tens, please?

Cashier: Certainly. So that's six ten pound ....⁷. Here you are.

Customer: Thank you. Goodbye.

6 Work in pairs. Practise the conversation in 5. Then change roles and practise again.

7 Role-play. Work in pairs. Take turns to be the customer and the bank cashier.
1 Arrange a transfer to your account.
2 Change some of your currency into dollars.
3 Cash a traveller's cheque.

Useful language
I'd like to arrange a transfer, please.
I'd like to send some money to an account in (Ireland).
I'd like to transfer (amount) from (my) account to (this) account.
The bank name is ... and the address is...
The account name is ... and the account number is...
How long will it take?
I'd like to change some money.
What's the rate?
What's the commission?

SF 2 SITUATIONS FILE
Health

1 Label the picture. Use the words in the box.

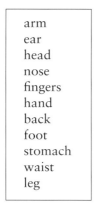

arm
ear
head
nose
fingers
hand
back
foot
stomach
waist
leg

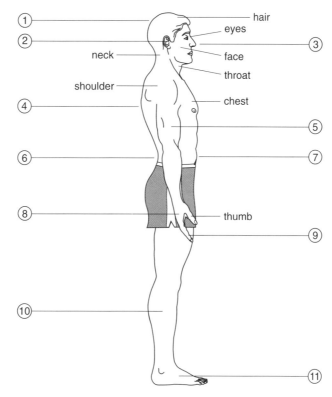

2 What's the problem? Match the problem with the picture.

1 I've got a headache. ....   5 I've got a hangover. ....

2 I've got a toothache. ....   6 I've got a cold. ....

3 I feel dizzy. ....   7 I feel sick. ....

4 I've got a sore throat. ....   8 I've got a pain in my leg. ....

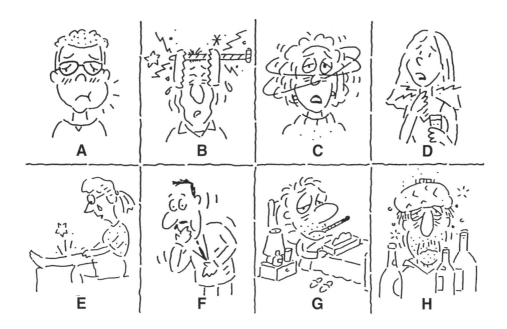

3 Who says the following sentences? Write D for doctor and
P for patient.

1 I'd like to make an appointment to see the doctor. ...

2 Take the tablets three times a day, before meals. ...

3 I've got aches and pains all over. ...

4 How long have you been feeling unwell? ...

5 I think I've got food poisoning. ...

6 Stay in bed for a few days. ...

7 You've got a virus. ...

8 I've sprained my ankle. ...

9 How long have you had a temperature? ...

10 I'll give you a prescription for antibiotics. ...

4 Work in pairs. Role-play this situation. Then change roles.

Student A You are the patient. Describe your symptoms to the doctor.

Student B You are the doctor. Ask your patient how long he/she has had the symptoms.
Give him/her advice, and a prescription if necessary.

5 Read the description of the health care system in the UK. Is it different from your country?
Describe how the system works in your country.

State health care in the UK

For medical problems, people consult their local GP (General Practitioner). Where necessary, the GP arranges an appointment with a specialist at a hospital. The patient does not pay for treatment from their GP or at a hospital.

You can buy medicines for minor problems at the chemist's without a doctor's prescription, for example, aspirin, cough mixture, vitamin pills. For other medicines, such as antibiotics, you need a prescription, and you pay a standard prescription charge.

Private health care

A growing number of people choose to pay for private health care because there is often a long waiting list to see specialists, and for non-urgent hospital operations in the state system. There are a number of private insurance schemes, which are often a perk for senior employees.

Giving directions

1 Look at the map below. You are at the George Hotel. Follow the instructions. Which places do you arrive at?

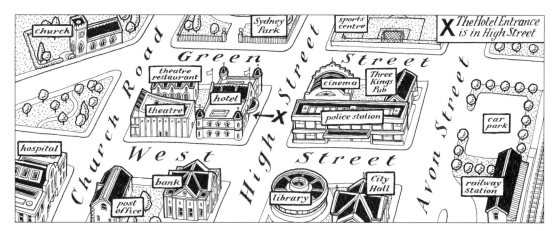

1 Turn right out of the hotel. Turn left into West Street. It's on the right, after the library.
2 Turn right out of the hotel, then right again. It's on the corner, opposite the post office.
3 Turn left out of the hotel, then turn first right. It's on the right, past the cinema.

2 Work in pairs. Ask for and give directions to the following places.
Use phrases from the box.

You are at the	You want to go to the
1 railway station	bank
2 car park	post office
3 City Hall	church
4 Theatre Restaurant	railway station
5 post office	Three Kings pub
6 sports centre	hospital

Useful language

Asking for directions

Excuse me, could you tell me | the way to...?
| how to get to...?

Giving directions

Turn | right out of the station...
| left when you come out of the bank...
Go along...
Walk to the end of...
Turn | first left...
| second right...
Cross the...
It's | at the beginning/end of Green Street, on the left/right.
| about half way along, just past the park.
| on the corner of West Street and Avon Street.
| in Church Road, opposite the hospital.
| in Green Street, next to the cinema.
| in High Street, after the bank.

3 Work in pairs. Describe how to get to the following.
Your home.
Your place of work.
Two places in your town or city.

Difficult situations: complaints and queries

1 Read the complaints and questions below.
Where is the speaker? What is the situation?

> 1
> I asked for a gin and tonic, not a gin and orange.

> 5
> I'm afraid this bread is stale.

> 9
> I think there's a mistake here. We had one bottle of wine, not two.

> 2
> I wanted to have a bath but there's no hot water.

> 6
> Do you have an express service? I need to have this suit cleaned as soon as possible.

> 10
> Excuse me, but you've taken my coat.

> 3
> I ordered the chicken, not the beef.

> 7
> I booked a room with a bath, not a shower.

> 11
> The shaver socket in my room doesn't work.

> 4
> You've given me the wrong change. I gave you a ten-pound note.

> 8
> Is it possible to remove this stain? I think it's red wine.

> 12
> Excuse me, but there's a queue.

Useful language

I asked for..., not...   You've...
Excuse me, but (there's a)...   Is it possible to...?
I'm afraid...

2 Work in pairs. What do you say in the following situations?

1 In a restaurant you order mushroom soup. The waiter brings you chicken soup.
2 In your hotel bathroom there is only one small towel.
3 At an underground station you ask for a £2 ticket. The clerk gives you a £1.50p ticket.
4 In a bar you ask for a glass of white wine. The bartender gives you red wine.
5 You take a jacket with a coffee stain to the dry-cleaner's. You need it the next day.
6 You are waiting in a queue in a bank. Somebody walks directly to the cash desk without queuing.
7 Someone picks up your coat in a restaurant.
8 Your hotel bedroom is too hot. You turned on the air-conditioning but nothing happened.
9 In a restaurant your wine glass is cracked and the fork is not clean.
10 You buy ten 25p stamps at a post office. You give the clerk a ten-pound note. He gives you £2.50p change.
11 The meat you order in a restaurant is undercooked.
12 When you check out of your hotel, the bill charges you for two breakfasts. You had one.

Monitor sheet

Date:

Language problems:

Useful words/phrases:

Check the pronunciation of these words:

TEST A   UNITS 1–4 Time limit 1 hour

A GRAMMAR

1 Present Simple and frequency adverbs
Put the words in the right order to make sentences or questions.

Example   go train usually they do by work to?
Do they usually go to work by train?

1 she usually appointments for is late.

2 always out they at go weekends do?

3 goes he restaurants lunch to for usually.

4 meetings he for never late is.

5 he abroad often travel business does on?

6 often you meet how abroad do visitors from?

7 always after tired work are they.

8 she rarely newspapers reads.

1 mark per answer   **Total 8**

2 Present Simple, Present Continuous and Past Simple
Complete the conversations. Use the correct form of the verb in brackets.

Richard is welcoming Nicole, a visitor from France.

1   **Richard:** .... you ....[1](have) a
     good flight?
     Nicole: Yes. The plane ....[2](leave)
     twenty minutes late but we ....[3]
     (arrive) on time.
     Richard: Good. .... you ....[4]
     (find) your way here easily?
     Nicole: Yes, I ....[5](take) a taxi from the
     airport.

2   **Richard:** Where .... you ....[6]
     (live) in France?
     Nicole: I ....[7](live) in central Paris, but I
     ....[8](not work) there. I ....[9]
     (work) in La Défense.
     Richard: Really? How .... you
     ....[10](travel) to work?
     Nicole: By train.
     Richard: And how long .... the journey
     ....[11](take)?
     Nicole: It's very quick. Only 20 minutes.

3   **Richard:** And what project .... you
     ....[12](work) on currently?
     Nicole: I ....[13](develop) a new computer
     system. It's only the beginning of the project
     so we ....[14](discuss) different
     possibilities at the moment. What about you?
     .... you ....[15](work) hard right
     now?
     Richard: Very hard at the moment because
     business ....[16](get) better.

1 mark per answer   **Total 16**

3 Present Simple or Past Simple
Complete the text. Use the correct form of the verb in brackets.

Ten years ago, Pietro Maldini ....[1](move) from Milan to the headquarters of his company in Paris. He ....[2](not live) in the city, but he ....[3](commute) to work by car every day. He ....[4](fly) to Milan regularly, and he ....[5](be) very happy with his life. When he ....[6](live) in Milan, he ....[7](not enjoy) his work, but now he ....[8](have) more responsibility and a good lifestyle. 'I am very happy I ....[9](make) the move when I did,' he says. 'My family and I ....[10](like) it here.'

1 mark per answer   **Total 10**

4 Irregular verbs
Write the past tense form of these verbs.

begin	get ....
buy	give ....
come	meet ....
choose	see ....
drink	spend ....
eat	think ....
find	write ....
fly	

1 mark per answer   **Total 15**

5 Question words
Match the questions and answers.

1 Where did you go?   a. Yesterday evening.

2 How often do you go   b. I rented a car.
  there?

3 Which airline did you   c. Because I didn't
  fly with?   sleep last night.

4 What did you do there?   d. To New York.

5 Which hotel did you   e. I went alone.
  stay at?

6 How did you travel to   f. About once a
  see your customers?   month.

7 What did you do in the   g. I visited our
  evenings?   important customers.

8 Who did you go with?   h. United Airlines.

9 When did you get back?   i. The Grand Hyatt
                                   Hotel.

10 Why are you tired?   j. I went out to
                                   restaurants.

1 mark per answer   **Total 10**

6 Comparative and superlative adjectives
Complete the chart.

Adjective	Comparative	Superlative
1 expensive	....	....
2 hot	....	....
3	....	least
4 happy	....	....
5	better	....
6 far	....	....
7 young	....	....
8 healthy	....	....
9	....	worst
10 exciting	....	....

½ mark per answer   **Total 10**

B   SOCIAL ENGLISH

1 Introductions, greetings, and goodbyes
Complete the conversations.

1 **You:** Excuse me, are you Jan Anson?
Jan: ....¹ right.
You: May I ....²? I'm (Paola Morgan).
   How do you do.
Jan: ....³.

2 **You:** Sue, I'd like ....⁴ a friend of mine,
   John Kelner.
Sue: Pleased to meet you, Mr Kelner.
John: How do you do. Please ....⁵ John.
Sue: Then you must call me Sue.

3 **You:** Hello Jan. Nice to see you again. How
   ....⁶?
Jan: Oh, fine, thanks. And you?
You: ....⁷.

4 **John:** Sue, I must go now. It was ....⁸,
   and I look forward to seeing you again.
Sue: I really enjoyed meeting you, too. Have a
   ....⁹ back.
John: Thank you and ....¹⁰ to you.
   Goodbye.

1 mark per answer   **Total 10**

2 Making contact
Complete the telephone conversations.

1 **Hotel receptionist:** Hotel President.
Rosa: ....¹ to James Turner, please.
Hotel receptionist: ....², please?
Rosa: Rosa Martinez.
Hotel receptionist: ....³ the line, please,
   Ms Martinez. I'll try his room.

2 **Hotel receptionist:** Hotel President.
Rosa: Mr Hutton, please.
Hotel receptionist: ....⁴ Mr Hutton isn't
   in at the moment.
Rosa: ....⁵ a message?

Hotel receptionist: Yes, of course.
Rosa: ....⁶ him to call me? My name's
   Martinez and my number's 347721.

1 mark per answer   **Total 6**

C   VOCABULARY
Read the clues and complete the word puzzle.

1	J
2	O
3	B
4	S
5	A
6	T
7	I
8	S
9	F
10	A
11	C
12	T
13	I
14	O
15	N

1   running slowly – a very popular sport
2   the opposite of *quieter*
3   a place for ships – Sydney has one of the
    world's loveliest of these
4   a water sport, using a small boat
5   Washington, Paris, and London are all
    .... cities
6   the number of people who live in a country, a
    city etc.
7   you put your clothes in this when you travel
8   the past tense of *speak*
9   the opposite of *dangerous*
10 a period where you have to wait longer than
    you expect, for example before a flight
11 the opposite of *more expensive*
12 'I'm afraid he's not in the office. Can I
    .... a message?'
13 not married
14 you clean your teeth with this
15 'Could you fill in this form and ....
    here, please.'

1 mark per answer   **Total 15**
TEST TOTAL 100

TEST B   UNITS 5 – 8   Time limit 1 hour

A   GRAMMAR

1 Mass and Count nouns

Are these nouns mass, count, or both? Write M (mass) C (count) or MC (mass and count).

....	information	....	news
....	exercise	....	wine
....	machine	....	job
....	nightlife	....	advice
....	people	....	work
....	problem	....	suitcase
....	luggage	....	time
....	unemployment	....	equipment
....	money	....	trip
....	machinery	....	food

½ mark per answer   **Total 10**

2 some/any/a lot (of)/much/many

Complete these sentences using *some/any/a lot (of)/much/many*.

1 How .... times have you been to South America?

2 I'm sure he's very rich. He's certainly got .... money.

3 Could you give me .... information about language courses, please?

4 There isn't .... industry in this area, only a few factories and workshops.

5 They didn't have .... tickets, but I managed to get two tickets for the concert.

6 We've bought .... machinery for the new factory, but we need to buy more.

7 I haven't got .... money. I've spent it all.

8 How .... time do you need for the project?

9 He didn't have .... problems with the language. He understood everything.

10 Would you like .... more coffee?

1 mark per answer   **Total 10**

3 for and since

Write *for* or *since*.

1	.... several years	6	.... the last three years
2	.... yesterday	7	.... last summer
3	.... ten days	8	.... twenty minutes
4	 1980	9	.... 6 a.m.
5	.... I was at school	10	.... a long time

1 mark per answer   **Total 10**

4 Irregular verbs

Complete the chart.

	Past	Past participle
do	....	....
eat	....	eaten
give	gave	....
make	....	....
study	....	....
write	....	....

1 mark per answer   **Total 10**

5 Present Perfect Simple or Past Simple

Complete the text. Use the correct form of the verb in brackets.

Richard ....[1](start) his career as an accountant with a multi-national firm ten years ago, and ....[2](be) with the same company ever since. He ....[3](have) several different positions in the company, and ....[4](work) in several different countries. Three years ago he ....[5](go) to work in Australia, and last year he ....[6](return) to the company's main office in London. He ....[7](like) living and working in Australia, and in the last few months he ....[8](find) it very difficult to adapt to living in Europe again. So last month he ....[9](decide) to start to look for a new job. So far, he ....[10](apply) for several jobs.

1 mark per answer   **Total 10**

6 Simple Past, Present Perfect Simple, and Present Perfect Continuous

Complete these questions from an interview. Use the correct form of the verb in brackets.

1 How long ago .... you .... (leave) university?

2 How many companies .... you .... (work) for since you .... (finish) university?

3 .... you .... (ever, have) any experience of managing a team of people?

4 How long .... you .... (work) for your present company?

5 What new responsibilities .... you .... (have) since you .... (start) your present job?

6 .... you .... (ever, go) to the Far East on business?

7 How many presentations .... you .... (give) in your present job?

8 How often .... you .... (speak) English in your job in the last six months?

1 mark per answer   **Total 10**

B SOCIAL ENGLISH

Complete the conversations with a suitable word or phrase.

1 Making and changing arrangements

1 **Nicole:** Alan, could we arrange a meeting to discuss the project?
   Alan: Yes, certainly. When .... ¹?
   Nicole: Is next Monday possible for you?
   Alan: No, ... ².
   Nicole: .... ³ Tuesday, then?
   Alan: Yes, that's fine.
   Nicole: Good, so I .... ⁴ meeting you on Tuesday then.

2 **Alan:** I'm very sorry, Nicole, but .... ⁵ the meeting on Tuesday. Could we .... ⁶?
   Nicole: Yes of course. When .... ⁷?
   Alan: What about Thursday morning?
   Nicole: Yes, ... ⁸.

2 Inviting

Ann: Mark, ... ⁹ to dinner with us next Saturday evening?

Mark: I'd love to come, Ann, but .... ¹⁰.

Ann: Oh, what a pity. .... ¹¹ the following Saturday instead?

Mark: Yes, ... ¹². Thank you.

3 Suggestions

John: We both need a holiday. .... ¹³ to Rome for a few days?

Gina: Oh no, we've been there before. .... ¹⁴ to a city we don't know – Prague for example.

John: Yes, ... ¹⁵. It's a very beautiful city.

Gina: We could go on Friday and return Monday evening.

John: OK, let's do that.

1 mark per answer **Total 15**

4 At a restaurant

Bart has invited Mary to a restaurant. Use the guide below to write their conversation.

Bart	Mary
Ask Mary what she would like.	Ask for a recommendation.
Recommend a starter/ main dish.	Say what you'd like.
Ask Mary what she'd like to drink.	Reply.
(Later)	
Offer a dessert/coffee.	Reply.
	(After meal)
Reply to thanks.	Thank Bart for the meal.

1 mark per answer **Total 10**

C VOCABULARY

Read the clues and complete the word puzzle.

```
 1 [ ][ ][ ][ ][F][ ][ ][ ]
          2 [L][ ][ ][ ]
 3 [Q][ ][ ][ ][I][ ][ ][ ][ ][ ]
      4 [A][ ][ ][G][ ][ ][ ]
        5 [B][ ][H][ ][ ]
 6 [C][ ][ ][ ][ ][T][ ][ ]
              7 [ ][A][ ][ ][ ]
          8 [ ][ ][T][ ][ ]
          9 [ ][ ][T][ ][ ]
         10 [ ][ ][E][ ][ ][ ]
11 [E][ ][ ][ ][N][ ][ ]
   12 [T][ ][ ][D][ ][ ][ ][ ]
           13 [ ][ ][A][ ][ ]
         14 [ ][ ][N][ ][ ]
15 [ ][ ][ ][ ][T][ ][ ]
```

1 you carry papers in this to work
2 'How ...., to win all that money!'
3 'Do you have the right .... for the job?'
4 'I .... for being so late. The traffic was terrible.'
5 a small book which gives pictures and information
6 the adjective of *competition*
7 smaller than an onion and good for your heart
8 you eat this before a main course
9 before a planes takes off, passengers hear .... instructions
10 you eat this after a main course
11 He got the job because he had a lot of useful ....
12 you feel this if you don't sleep, or after a long flight
13 'I'm very sorry. I have to .... our meeting on Thursday.'
14 another word for *advantage*
15 you often hear .... announcements at airports

1 mark per answer **Total 15**
TEST TOTAL 100

TEST C   UNITS 9 – 12   Time limit 1 hour

A   GRAMMAR

1 Irregular verbs
Complete the chart.

	Past	Past participle
build	....	....
drink	....	....
fall	....	....
grow	....	....
lose	....	....
put	....	....

1 mark per answer   **Total 12**

2 Passives
Make sentences or questions with the passive in the Present Simple, Past Simple, or Present Perfect.

Example   On what occasions / champagne / drink?
On what occasions is champagne drunk?

1   How / champagne / make / today?
....

2   When / *la méthode champenoise* / first / discover?
....

3   Which grapes / use / to make champagne?
....

4   The cellars under Champagne / use / to store champagne / since Roman times.
....

5   Strong champagne bottles / first / make / in the 17th century.
....

6   How long ago / chocolate / introduce / to Europe?
....

7   How much chocolate / eat / today in Britain?
....

8   When / coffee / introduce / to Europe?
....

9   10.5 kilos of coffee / buy / by Scandinavians every year.
....

10   Recently new types of instant coffee / create / for the mass market.
....

1 mark per answer   **Total 10**

3 Modals
Complete these sentences with *must*, *mustn't*, or *needn't*.

1   In this country you can drive with your national driving licence. You .... have an international driving licence.

2   It isn't possible to enter the country without a passport, so you .... have a valid passport when you travel there.

3   You can go to prison if you drink alcohol and drive, so you .... drink if you're going to drive.

4   You can enter the country without a visa, so you .... get a visa before you travel.

Complete these sentences with *should*, *shouldn't*, *may*, or *might*.

5   People usually dress formally for work so you .... do the same, although it's not absolutely necessary!

6   It doesn't happen very often but your host .... invite you to dinner at his home.

7   For invitations, it's not usual to arrive exactly on time, but you .... be more than about ten minutes late.

8   I think cotton clothes are best. You .... find synthetic clothes uncomfortable in the hot, tropical climate.

1 mark per answer   **Total 8**

4 First Conditional
Complete the sentences. Use the correct form of the verb in brackets.

1   If I .... (see) Tom tomorrow, I .... (give) him the news.

2   You .... (miss) the plane if you .... (not leave) now.

3   If he .... (accept) the new job, his salary .... (increase)?

4   They .... (change) the system if there .... (be) any more problems.

5   If we .... (not send) the package today, it .... (not arrive) before Monday.

1 mark per answer   **Total 10**

5 Second Conditional
Read the text about Sue and complete the sentences below.

Sue is not very happy at present. She works long hours and gets home late every evening. She never goes out in the evening because she's always very tired. She's not very healthy, either, because she doesn't do any sport. Her friends don't invite her out because she never accepts their invitations. She knows the only solution is to find an interesting job nearer her home.

1   If Sue .... shorter hours, she .... home earlier every evening.

2   She .... out in the evenings if she .... so tired.

3   She .... healthier if she .... some sport.

© Oxford University Press

4   If she .... their invitations, her friends
    .... her out.

5   If she .... an interesting job nearer her
    home, she .... a lot happier.

1 mark per answer   **Total 10**

B   SOCIAL ENGLISH

1 Offers and requests

Write the offers and requests for these situations,
and the responses to them.

1   Bob asks Rosa to lend him her car. Rosa refuses
    and gives a reason.
    ....

2   Rosa asks Bob to help her translate a report
    into English. Bob agrees.
    ....

3   Rosa offers to meet Bob at the airport. He
    accepts.
    ....

4   Bob offers to get some travel information for
    Rosa. She declines.
    ....

2 marks per answer   **Total 8**

2 Asking for information

Write indirect questions, beginning with the
phrases given.

1   What's the rail fare from Paris to Milan?
    Could you tell me .... ?

2   Can I buy my ticket on the train?
    Do you know if .... ?

3   Do I need to make a reservation?
    Can you tell me if .... ?

4   How long does the journey take?
    Could you tell me .... ?

5   Is there a dining car on the train?
    Do you know if .... ?

6   How many trains a day are there?
    Can you tell me .... ?

7   Is the service the same at the weekend?
    I'd like to know ....

8   Which platform does the train leave from?
    Can you tell me .... ?

9   What time is the next train?
    Do you know .... ?

10 When does it arrive in Milan?
    Can you tell me .... ?

1 mark per answer   **Total 10**

3 Social responses

Write suitable responses for these statements and
questions.

1   A Have a good weekend.
    B ....

2   A Could I use your phone?
    B ....

3   A I failed my final exam.
    B ....

4   A I'm sorry I'm late. The traffic was very bad.
    B ....

5   A Do you mind if I open the window?
    B ....

6   A May I sit here?
    B ....

7   A Thank you for all your help.
    B ....

8   A Could you pass the bread, please?
    B ....

9   A I've just been offered a really good job.
    B ....

10 A Can I get you a coffee?
    B ....

1 mark per answer   **Total 10**

4 Thanking for hospitality and saying goodbye

Write what you would say in these situations.

1   On a business trip your host invited you to his
    home for dinner one evening. What do say as
    you leave after dinner?
    ....

2   Some people you have met on holiday invited
    you to a barbecue party on the beach. What do
    you say as you leave after the barbecue?
    ....

3   You're at a party with friends. It's very late
    and you have to go to work the next day.
    What do you say to your friends as you leave?
    ....

4   A meeting at work is running late. Your plane
    is leaving very soon. What do you say as you
    leave the meeting?
    ....

5   A friend has given you a lift to your English
    class. What do you say as you get out of the car?
    ....

1 mark per answer   **Total 5**

C VOCABULARY

Read the clues and complete the word puzzle.

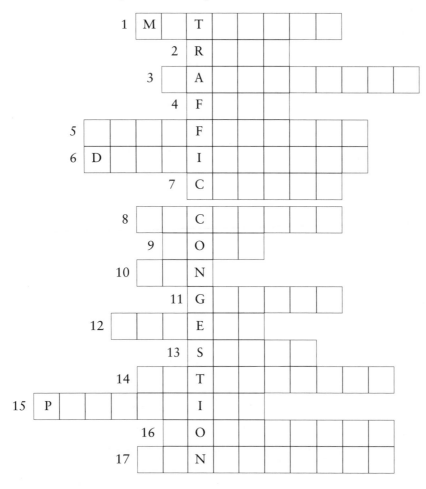

1 a person who drives a car

2 the opposite of *polite*

3 you use this to calculate quickly

4 the price of a journey by bus, train, etc.

5 the opposite of *efficient*

6 the place you are going to

7 a room underground for storing wine, etc.

8 the noun of *recover*

9 a period when a country's economy is doing very well

10 many people want to .... traffic from city centres

11 wine is made from this fruit

12 a TV and a computer monitor have this

13 another word for *recession*

14 the noun of *retire*

15 traffic causes this in cities

16 we all buy products and services – we are all
....

17 a word which means *on time*

1 mark per answer   Total 17
TEST TOTAL 100

© Oxford University Press

RESOURCE FILE
ANSWER KEY

1.4 1 apartment – flat
drugstore – chemist's
elevator – lift
subway – underground
restroom – toilet
round trip – return

2 cab – taxi
freeway – motorway
movie theater – cinema
fall – autumn
pants – trousers
sidewalk – pavement

3 **British**   **American**
colour   check
theatre   catalog
programme   traveler

4 favourite
litre
dialogue
centre
labour

1.6 1
1 salary	7 daughter
2 spell	8 commute
3 repeat	9 leisure
4 colleagues	10 translator
5 vineyard	11 flat
6 single	12 suburbs

2
1 swimming	4 sailing
2 walking	5 horse-riding
3 cycling	6 jogging

2.1 Permanent or long-term situations: He works for an international company, We export to France and Spain, My journey to work takes about 45 minutes.
Routine activities: I usually play tennis at weekends, I don't often make business trips abroad, I sometimes visit trade fairs.
Activities happening at the time of speaking: He's talking to a customer at the moment, Mr Bell is having lunch with a customer, The sales manager is making a presentation.
Temporary situations or events in progress: I'm taking the train to work this month, Our company is entering new markets, Competition in the airline industry is growing.

2.2 1 Peter often makes business trips to the USA.
2 When do you usually start work?
3 How often do you come here?
4 He is talking to a visitor at the moment.
5 I never play tennis in the winter.
6 I have four weeks' holiday every year.
7 He is never late.
8 We are doing a lot of extra work this week.
9 Currently our sales are increasing.
10 I always travel to work by car.

2.6
1 hold	7 range
2 message	8 turnover
3 attend	9 currently
4 products	10 employees
5 quality	11 presentation
6 customers	12 suppliers

3.1 1 I didn't go on holiday last year.
2 When did you buy your car?
3 Who did you meet at the party?
4 How much did you pay for the ticket?
5 Stephen and Martyn didn't come to work yesterday.
6 When did you start to play golf?
7 Why didn't you come on time?
8 Sales didn't increase last year.
9 What time did he start work last week?
10 How often did they visit you?

3.4 1
attend a conference	rent a car
book a hotel	stay at a hotel
book a table	take photos
celebrate an anniversary	visit a museum
do some sightseeing	

3
Across
1 motorway	6 link
2 spectators	7 advantages
3 climate	8 project
4 delay	9 discovery
5 location	

Down
1 meeting	4 success
2 career	5 taxpayers
3 viewers	

4
Across: cost, went, flew, came
Down: thought, won, met, took, ate, read, drank, saw

4.3 1 Contact reception.
2 Early morning call.
3 On the back of the hotel door.
4 No (they are complimentary).
5 Between 7.00 a.m. and 11.00 p.m.
6 Yes.
7 Dial 9.
8 0.

5.2 1
a slice of salami	a jar of marmalade
a glass of wine	a bowl of sugar
a bottle of water	a piece of cake
a packet of peanuts	a bunch of grapes
a tube of tomato paste	a can of cola
a box of matches	a carton of milk

2
a bottle/glass of wine, water, beer, orange juice, cola
a packet of sugar, peanuts, biscuits, cigarettes,

rice
a slice of salami, cake, bread, cheese, meat
a bowl of sugar, milk, fruit, strawberries, salad
a piece of cake, bread, cheese, meat
a can of cola, beer, orange juice
a jar of jam, honey, marmalade
a carton of milk, yoghurt, orange juice
a bunch of grapes, flowers
a box of matches, chocolates
a tube of tomato paste, toothpaste

6.1 1

1 I flew to the USA three weeks ago.
2 In your life, how many different countries have you lived in?
3 In his present job, he travels to Europe every month.
4 When did you see her the last time?
5 He's not here. He's gone to Mexico.
6 I went to Tokyo twice last month.
7 She has done a lot of work in the last few days.
8 I bought a new car last week.
9 How many hours have you worked so far this week?
10 How long ago did you go to university?

2

1 American. I've just had an interview.
2 British. Did you phone the bank yet?
3 American. They've already seen the film.
4 American. I haven't received your letter yet.

6.5

1	consultant	9	worldwide
2	applicant	10	cruises
3	brochure	11	experience
4	trainee	12	interviewee
5	decade	13	creative
6	corporate	14	catalogue
7	application	15	short-list
8	energetic		

7.1 Past events

I met Anton three years ago.
He bought his car this time last year.
She qualified as a doctor in 1992.
I bought my computer two years ago.
She started her present job six months ago.
They got married in 1990.
Pete started work as a teacher in January last year.
I got this Walkman a long time ago.
We moved to our flat last month.
He became a translator when he left university.

Past–Present situations

I've known Anton for three years.
He's owned his car for a year.
She's been a doctor since 1992.
I've had my computer for two years.
They've been married since 1990.
She's had her present job for six months.
He's been a teacher for over a year.

I've had this Walkman for ages.
We've been in our flat since last month.
He's been a translator since he left university.

7.2

1 I've had my car for a long time.
2 How long have you been working for your company?
3 I've known your sister for a long time.
4 How many cigarettes have you smoked this morning?
5 I've been living here since 1992.
6 How long has she had her job?
7 How many years have you been teaching English?
8 How long have they been members of the golf club?
9 He's worked for the same company for ages.
10 Our business has been doing very well since last year.

7.4

1	abroad	6	fortunes
2	labour costs	7	headhunter
3	freelance	8	deficit
4	surplus	9	responsibilities
5	celebration	10	boom

8.4

arrivals board	hand luggage
airport terminal	landing card
aisle seat	life jacket
baggage claim	luggage trolley
boarding card	overhead locker
check-in desk	passport control
departures board	safety instructions
duty-free allowance	seat belt
duty-free shop	security announcement
flight announcement	security check
flight attendant	window seat

9.3 1

1 d., 2 f., 3 e., 4 a., 5 h., 6 b., 7 i., 8 j., 9 c., 10 g.

9.3 2

1 printer 2 CD-Rom drive 3 monitor
4 screen 5 disk drive 6 mouse 7 keyboard
8 calculator 9 floppy disk

10.1

1 invited, would you wear
2 asked, would you buy
3 had, would you buy
4 would you study, gave
5 would you choose, went
6 would you buy, gave
7 would you pack
8 would you go, offered
9 had, would you choose
10 would you go
11 would you study, offered
12 would you do, was/were
13 would you spend, were
14 would you do, could
15 changed, would you do
16 would you choose, asked
17 offered, would you accept
18 were, would you spend
19 would you say, asked
20 would you prepare, asked

10.2 1
1 a., 2 d., 3 i., 4 e., 5 b., 6 f.

2
1 b., 2 e., 3 a., 4 g., 5 d., 6 c., 7 f.

10.3
2	to estimate	8	a silencer
3	to suffer	9	a whistle
4	huge	10	chaos
5	to make a complaint	11	to install
6	a siren	12	to monitor
7	a horn		

11.1 1
development	tiredness
improvement	happiness
announcement	fitness
requirement	sadness
achievement	kindness
government	stiffness
possibility	explanation
popularity	connection
reality	reduction
punctuality	description
security	reservation
activity	cancellation

12.1 1
1d., 2e., 3b., 4c., 5a.

2
1 are chosen
2 is spread, are used
3 is drawn, is lost
4 is wiped, is left
5 is washed, is spread
6 is put, are regulated
7 is left
8 is distributed, is sold

12.2
1	are killed	7	was reduced
2	was founded	8	were started
3	have been killed	9	are introduced
4	have been injured	10	will be forced
5	have been made	11	will be reduced
6	were introduced		

SF1 1
1 bank notes
2 traveller's cheques
3 cash dispenser
4 account number
5 eurocheque
6 coins
7 plastic cards
8 exchange rates

3
I'd like to cash some traveller's cheques, please.
Certainly. Have you got any identification on you?
Yes, here's my passport.
Would you sign each cheque, please?
Fine. Can I borrow your pen?
Thank you. That's fine. How would you like the money?

Three ten, and four five-pound notes, please.
Right. That's three ten-pound notes and four fives. Fifty pounds in total.

5
1	to cash	5	signature
2	guarantee card	6	card number
3	amount	7	notes
4	date		

SF2 1
1	head	7	stomach
2	ear	8	hand
3	nose	9	fingers
4	back	10	leg
5	arm	11	foot
6	waist		

2 1b., 2a., 3c., 4d.,
5h., 6g., 7f., 8e.

3
1	P	6	D
2	D	7	D
3	P	8	P
4	D	9	D
5	P	10	D

SF3 1
1 City Hall
2 Theatre
3 Three Kings pub

Test A

A1
1 She is usually late for appointments.
2 Do they always go out at weekends?
3 He usually goes to restaurants for lunch.
4 He is never late for meetings.
5 Does he often travel abroad on business?
6 How often do you meet visitors from abroad?
7 They are always tired after work.
8 She rarely reads newspapers.

A2
1 1 Did you have, 2 left, 3 arrived,
4 Did you find, 5 took
2 6 Do you live, 7 live, 8 don't work,
9 work, 10 do you travel, 11 does the journey take
3 12 are you working, 13 am developing,
14 are discussing, 15 Are you working,
16 is getting

A3
1 moved, 2 doesn't live, 3 commutes,
4 flies, 5 is, 6 lived, 7 didn't enjoy, 8 has,
9 made, 10 like

A4
began bought came chose drank ate
found flew got gave met saw spent
thought wrote

A5
1 d., 2 f., 3h., 4g., 5i., 6b., 7j., 8e., 9a., 10c.

A6

1 expensive – more expensive – most expensive
2 hot – hotter – hottest
3 little – less – least
4 happy – happier – happiest
5 good – better – best
6 far – farther – farthest (further – furthest)
7 young – younger – youngest
8 healthy – healthier – healthiest
9 bad – worse – worst
10 exciting – more exciting – most exciting

B1

1 1 That's
   2 introduce myself
   3 How do you do
2 4 you to meet
   5 call me
3 6 are you
   7 Very well, thanks/Fine, thanks/
     Not too bad, thanks
4 8 very nice meeting you
   9 good trip/journey/flight
  10 the same

B2

1 1 I'd like to speak/Could I speak
   2 Who's calling
   3 Hold
2 4 I'm afraid
   5 Could you take
   6 Could you ask

C

1	jogging	9	safe
2	noisier	10	delay
3	harbour	11	cheaper
4	sailing	12	take
5	capital	13	single
6	population	14	toothpaste
7	suitcase	15	sign
8	spoke		

Test B

A1

information M   news M   exercise M or C
wine M   machine C   job C   nightlife M
advice M   people C   work M   problem C
suitcase C   luggage M   time M
unemployment M   equipment M
money M   trip C   machinery M   food M

A2

1	many	6	some
2	a lot of	7	any
3	some	8	much
4	much	9	any
5	many	10	some

A3

1	for	6	for
2	since	7	since
3	for	8	for
4	since	9	since
5	since	10	for

A4

do – did – done
eat – ate – eaten
give – gave – given
make – made – made
study – studied – studied
write – wrote – written

A5

1	started	6	returned
2	has been	7	liked
3	has had	8	has found
4	has worked	9	decided
5	went	10	has applied

A6

1 did you leave
2 have you worked, finished
3 Have you ever had
4 have you worked/have you been working
5 have you had, started
6 Have you ever been
7 have you given
8 have you spoken

B1

1 1 would be convenient for you/could we
     meet/are you free/would suit you
   2 I'm afraid I'm busy then/I've got
     another appointment then
   3 How about
   4 look forward to
2 5 I'm afraid I can't manage/I have to
     cancel
   6 arrange another time
   7 would be convenient for you
   8 that's fine

B2

 9 would you like to come
10 I'm afraid I can't
11 How about
12 I'd love to/I'd enjoy that

B3

13 How about going/Why don't we go
14 I suggest we go/We could go
15 let's do that/that's a good idea

B4

(possible answers)
What would you like?
What do you recommend?
The (corned beef) is usually excellent here.
I'll have (the corned beef).
What would you like to drink?
A glass of (water).

Would you like a dessert?/coffee?
Yes. That would be very nice.

Thank you for a really excellent meal.
Don't mention it.

C

1	briefcase	9	safety
2	lucky	10	dessert
3	qualifications	11	experience
4	apologize	12	tiredness
5	brochure	13	cancel
6	competitive	14	benefit
7	garlic	15	security
8	starter		

Test C

A1

build – built – built
drink – drank – drunk
fall – fell – fallen
grow – grew – grown
lose – lost – lost
put – put – put

A2

1 How is champagne made today?
2 When was *la méthode champenoise* first discovered?
3 Which grapes are used to make champagne?
4 The cellars under Champagne have been used to store champagne since Roman times.
5 Strong champagne bottles were first made in the 17th century.
6 How long ago was chocolate introduced to Europe?
7 How much chocolate is eaten today in Britain?
8 When was coffee introduced to Europe?
9 10.5 kilos of coffee are bought by Scandinavians every year.
10 Recently new types of instant coffee have been created for the mass market.

A3

1	needn't	5	should
2	must	6	might
3	mustn't	7	shouldn't
4	needn't	8	may/might

A4

1 see, will give
2 will miss, don't leave
3 accepts, will his salary increase
4 will change, are
5 don't send, won't arrive

A5

1 worked, would get
2 would go, weren't (wasn't)
3 would be, did
4 accepted, would invite
5 had/found, would be

B1

(possible answers)
1 Could you lend me your car?
   I'm afraid not, I need it.

2 Do you think you could help me translate this report?
   Yes. Certainly.
3 Would you like me to meet you at the airport?
   Thank you. I'd appreciate that.
4 Do you want me to get you some travel information?
   Thanks, but please don't bother.

B2

1 Could you tell me what the rail fare from Paris to Milan is?
2 Do you know if I can buy my ticket on the train?
3 Can you tell me if I need to make a reservation?
4 Could you tell me how long the journey takes?
5 Do you know if there is a dining car on the train?
6 Can you tell me how many trains there are a day?
7 I'd like to know if the service is the same at the weekend.
8 Can you tell me which platform the train leaves from?
9 Do you know what time the next train is?
10 Can you tell me what time it arrives in Milan?

B3

(possible answers)

1	Thanks. You too.	6	Please do.
2	Yes, of course.	7	You're welcome.
3	I'm sorry to hear that.	8	Yes, here you are.
4	Never mind.	9	Congratulations!
5	No, not at all.	10	Thanks.

B4

(possible answers)
1 Thank you very much for your hospitality. I really appreciated it.
2 Thank you for inviting me. I've had a wonderful time.
3 I must go now.
4 I must be off. I look forward to seeing you again.
5 Thanks a lot. See you soon.

C

1	motorist	10	ban
2	rude	11	grapes
3	calculator	12	screen
4	fare	13	slump
5	inefficient	14	retirement
6	destination	15	pollution
7	cellar	16	consumers
8	recovery	17	punctually
9	boom		

Oxford University Press,
Great Clarendon Street, Oxford OX2 6DP

Oxford New York
Athens Auckland Bangkok Bogotá Buenos Aires
Cape Town Chennai Dar es Salaam Delhi
Florence Hong Kong Istanbul Karachi Kolkata
Kuala Lumpur Madrid Melbourne Mexico City
Mumbai Nairobi Paris São Paulo Shanghai
Singapore Taipei Tokyo Toronto Warsaw

and associated companies in
Berlin Ibadan

OXFORD and OXFORD ENGLISH
are trade marks of Oxford University Press

ISBN 0 19 435652 3

© Oxford University Press 1996

First published 1996
Fifth impression 2001

Photocopying

Printed in Hong Kong

Acknowledgements

The author and publisher would like to thank all those who worked with
and commented on the pilot version of these materials for their invaluable
help. Especial thanks are due to Tracy Byrne, Jane McKinlay, and Jacqui
Robinson for their comments and feedback on the manuscript.

The publishers and author would like to thank the following for their kind
permission to use adapted extracts from copyright material:
British Airways and **Premier Magazines** for extracts from *High Life* in-flight
magazine.
EuroBusiness Magazine for extracts from an article by Nicola White from
EuroBusiness.
The European Limited for extracts from six articles from *The European*.
Legal and General Assurance Society Limited for extracts from 'The Legal
and General Value of a Wife Report', February 1993.

Illustrations by Neil Gower, Alex Tiani, Technical Graphics OUP

Photography by Stephen Oliver